THE BASICS OF PISTOL SHOOTING

[handwritten notes:]

Matching en gun + ammunition

Know your Ammo
primers + diff component
Fundamentals
misfires
hangfires
squib loads

hand position
components of
grip
breath control
Site picture

you may bring your own
guns next wk

Produced by the Community Service Programs Division and the
Education and Training Division

A Publication of the National Rifle Association of America

First Edition—January, 1991

©1991 The National Rifle Association of America

13270   04/03

ACKNOWLEDGMENTS

The Community Service Programs Division and the Education and Training Division of the National Rifle Association of America gratefully acknowledge the significant contributions of the following persons who generously volunteered their time, knowledge, and skills in the preparation of this book:

Dr. Nathan R. Arenson-Chairman, NRA Pistol Committee; member, NRA Board of Directors; member, NRA Executive Committee; former president, Florida State Pistol Association; Distinguished Pistol Shot; four-time Florida Civilian Pistol Champion.

Mr. Billie R. McElroy-Retired Firearm Training Officer, Texas Department of Public Safety; former Texas Highway Patrolman; member, NRA Board of Directors; member, NRA Education and Training Committee; Distinguished Pistol Shot; member, 2600 Club (conventional pistol); member, 1480 Club (police pistol combat).

Mr. Leonard H. Pinaud-Police firearm instructor; NRA Training Counselor Workshop volunteer; NRA certified class C rifle coach; NRA certified instructor for all shooting disciplines.

Mr. Harry Reeves-Retired Inspector, Detroit Police Department; Vice Chairman, NRA Pistol Committee; member, NRA Board of Directors; six-time NRA National Pistol Champion; World Center-fire Champion (1952); seven-time World and Pan-American medalist; manager and coach of four Pan-American and U.S. Olympic Shooting Teams; member, International Shooting Union (UIT) Pistol Committee.

Col. Walter R. Walsh-Retired USMC; former Special Agent, Federal Bureau of Investigation; U.S. Marine Corps Pistol Champion (1946); Olympian, 50-meter free pistol (1948); Distinguished Pistol Shot; U.S. Olympic Shooting Team Captain (1972).

Mr. Joseph C. White-Retired official, U.S. Immigration and Naturalization Service; former Chief of Air Operations, U.S. Border Patrol; former member, NRA Pistol Committee; Chairman, NRA Competition Rules and Programs Committee; member, NRA Board of Directors; six-time National Senior Pistol Champion; member, 2650 Club (conventional pistol).

C O N T E N T S

INTRODUCTION

The word *pistol* may have come from the name of a small town, Pistoia, in northern Italy, where handguns were manufactured in the 15th and 16th centuries. However, some scholars attribute its origin to the Russian word for a 15th century matchlock gun—*pischal*. And other researchers believe that the word may derive from the Czechoslovakian word *pistala*, or pipe. Regardless of the true origin of the word, a common definition today for the word *pistol* is a gun that has a short barrel and can be held, aimed, and fired with one hand.

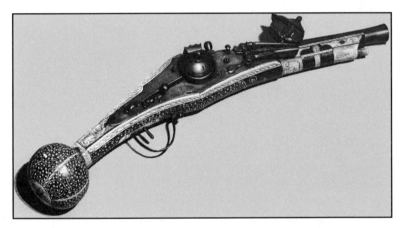

Many different types of pistols exist, including revolvers, semi-automatics, muzzleloaders, hinged actions, bolt-actions, and air pistols. Although the word *pistol* is frequently associated only with semi-automatic handguns, it is proper to use *pistol* to refer to all types of handguns.

This book will deal primarily with the two types of pistols in most common use today: the revolver and the semi-automatic.

Although muzzleloading pistols are not covered in this book, the sport of shooting these unique pistols is rapidly increasing in popularity. To learn about these pistols, see the NRA's publication *The Muzzleloading Pistol Handbook* (# 14350). The "NRA Publications" section (Appendix F) at the end of this book contains information for ordering NRA publications.

Air pistol shooting is also a very popular activity. This type of shooting can provide a wide variety of recreation and sport opportunities—from shooting in a basement or backyard range to competing in the Olympic Games. For a brief discussion of air pistols, see Appendix B.

Americans own pistols today for a wide variety of reasons. Some people own pistols for personal protection. Other persons fire pistols in competitive shooting tournaments held throughout the country, including matches on the collegiate and Olympic level. Hunters are finding that the use of handguns can be a challenging and exciting experience, and 47 of the 50 states permit handgun hunting.

A new shooter will quickly discover that pistol shooting is definitely fun! It's a sport that requires good hand and eye coordination, plus mental concentration and discipline. The purpose of this book is to teach the safe and proper use of a pistol so that it can be enjoyed to the fullest extent.

Some of the subjects covered in this handbook are: pistol parts and terms, types of ammunition, operation of various pistol actions, safety, cleaning, storage, and learning how to properly shoot a pistol. Keep this book in a handy place—it's a valuable guide that can be referred to again and again.

CHAPTER 1

| PISTOL PARTS AND OPERATION |

A pistol is a mechanical device and, as with any machine, it is necessary to understand how it works before it can be safely used and its operation mastered. In the hands of a responsible, knowledgeable, and safety-conscious person, a pistol is safe and reliable. (See Chapter 3 of this book for a discussion and explanation of gun safety rules.)

In order to begin to understand how a pistol works, the names and definitions of the various types of pistols and pistol parts must first be learned.

TYPES OF PISTOLS

The two most common types of pistols in use today are the *revolver* and the *semi-automatic*.

A pistol consists of three major components: the *frame*, the *barrel*, and the *action*.

Although both revolvers and semi-automatics have these three components, some of the parts within these components and the ways in which they function are different. These differences will be explained in this section.

REVOLVERS

BASIC OPERATION

A revolver is a pistol that has a rotating cylinder designed to contain cartridges. The action of the trigger and/or hammer will rotate the cylinder and fire a cartridge. To understand how this firing process occurs and how to safely load and unload cartridges, it is necessary to first become familiar with the names and functions of the various parts of a revolver.

REVOLVER COMPONENTS

Frame

The *frame* of the revolver is the backbone to which all other parts are attached.

1

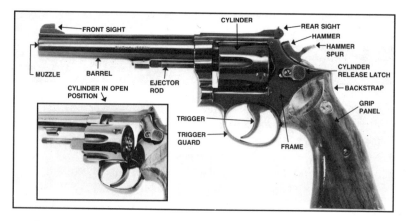

Grip panels are attached to the lower rear portion of the frame. Grip panels are usually composed of wood, rubber, or molded plastic, and are attached to the frame with screws.

The *backstrap* is the rear, vertical portion of the frame that lies between the grip panels.

The *trigger guard* is located on the underside of the frame and is designed to protect the trigger in order to reduce the possibility of an unintentional firing.

On top of the frame is the *rear sight* which is used in the aiming process.

Barrel

The *barrel* is the metal tube through which a bullet passes on its way to a target.

The inside of the barrel is called the *bore*. The bore has spiral *grooves* cut into it. The ridges of metal between these grooves are called *lands*. Together, the grooves and lands make up what is known as *rifling*.

Rifling makes the bullet spin as it leaves the barrel so that it will be more stable in flight and therefore travel more accurately. The distance between the lands determines the *caliber* of the pistol.

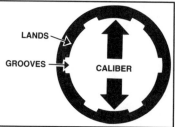

This distance is measured in hundredths of an inch (such as .22 caliber or .45 caliber) or in millimeters (such as 7.65mm or 9mm). The front end of the barrel where the bullet exits is called the *muzzle*.

The *front sight* is located on top of the barrel near the muzzle, and together with the rear sight is used to aim the pistol.

Action

The *action* is a group of moving parts used to load, fire, and unload the pistol. The parts of the action are attached to the frame of the revolver.

The *trigger* is located on the underside of the frame. The *hammer* is attached to the rear of the frame. When the trigger is pulled, it activates the hammer which in turn causes the *firing pin* to strike and fire the cartridge. In some revolvers, the firing pin is attached to the hammer; in other models, it is located inside the frame.

In *single-action* revolvers, the trigger performs only one action—releasing the hammer. The trigger does not cock the hammer. The hammer must be cocked with the thumb, and will stay in a cocked position to the rear of the frame until it is released by pulling the trigger.

In *double-action* revolvers, the trigger performs two tasks. When it is pulled, it will cock *and* release the hammer, firing the pistol. Most double-action revolvers can also be fired in a single-action mode by manually cocking the hammer with the thumb. The hammer will then stay in the cocked position until it is released by pulling the trigger.

The *cylinder* holds cartridges in individual *chambers* which are arranged in a circular pattern. (Cylinders usually contain five or six chambers.) Each time that the hammer moves to the rear, the cylinder turns and brings a new chamber in line with the barrel and the firing pin.

The *cylinder release latch* found on many revolvers releases the cylinder and allows it to swing out so that cartridges can be loaded and unloaded.

3

Most revolvers have an *ejector* (also known as an *extractor*) and/or an *ejector rod*. Although the operation and location of ejectors and ejector rods may vary, the purpose is the same—to remove cartridges from the cylinder.

SEMI-AUTOMATICS

BASIC OPERATION

A semi-automatic pistol differs significantly from a revolver in its basic operation. After a cartridge is fired by pulling the trigger, the empty case is automatically extracted and ejected, and a new cartridge is inserted into the chamber. (Because a new cartridge is automatically "loaded" or placed into the chamber, this type of pistol is sometimes referred to as an *autoloader*.)

SEMI-AUTOMATIC COMPONENTS

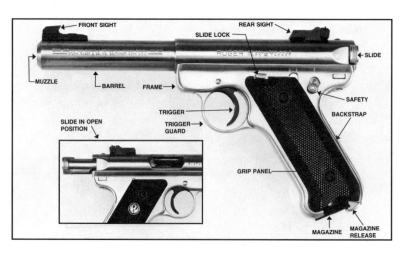

Although the basic operation of a semi-automatic pistol differs from that of a revolver, a semi-automatic has the same three major components: the *frame*, the *barrel*, and the *action*.

Frame

The *frame* of a semi-automatic pistol, like that of a revolver, is the backbone to which all other parts are attached.

4

The *safety* is located on the semi-automatic frame. (Revolvers do not usually have safeties.) The safety is a mechanical device designed to reduce the chance of an accidental discharge. Since safeties, like all mechanical devices, can malfunction, the prevention of an accident is ultimately the responsibility of the individual who is handling the pistol.

The *slide stop* (also known as a *slide lock* or *slide release*) is designed to hold the *slide* of the semi-automatic pistol to the rear. (See "Action" section below for a discussion of the slide.)

Some semi-automatics also have a part known as a *decocking lever*, which is used to lower the hammer and/or uncock the pistol.

Grip panels are attached to the lower rear portion of the frame. Grip panels are usually composed of wood, rubber, or molded plastic, and are attached to the frame with screws.

The *backstrap* is the rear, vertical portion of the frame that lies between the grip panels.

The *trigger guard* is located on the underside of the frame and is designed to protect the trigger in order to reduce the possibility of an unintentional firing.

Barrel

The *barrel* is the metal tube through which a bullet passes on its way to a target. The front end of the barrel where the bullet exits is called the *muzzle*, and the inside of the barrel is called the *bore*.

The barrel on a semi-automatic pistol is basically the same as the barrel on a revolver with one major exception: at the rear of the barrel on a semi-automatic is a *single chamber* which will contain the cartridge at the instant of firing. In contrast, the revolver has multiple chambers which are located in the cylinder.

Action

Because of the large number of different mechanical designs for semi-automatics, the actions can vary greatly. Some semi-automatics have a *hammer* that strikes a *firing pin*. Models which do not have a visible hammer are commonly referred to as *hammerless*, even though a hammer may actually be part of an *internal firing mechanism*. And some internal firing mechanisms may be designed without a hammer. Because of these variations,

5

the instruction manual for the pistol must be carefully read and understood before using the pistol. If questions still exist after reading the manual, consult a knowledgeable person.

All semi-automatics have a *slide*. On some models, the slide fits around the barrel, while on other models it is located at the rear of the barrel. In all semi-automatics, the first cartridge must always be manually cycled into the firing chamber by retracting the slide and then releasing it. As the slide returns to the closed position, it removes a cartridge from the top of the magazine and inserts it into the chamber.

The *front sight* and *rear sight* are usually located on the top of the slide, although in some models the sights may be located on the top of the barrel or on the top of the frame.

The *magazine* is a storage device designed to hold cartridges ready for insertion into the chamber. The *magazine release* is a device that releases the magazine so that it can be removed from the pistol.

The *trigger* is located on the underside of the frame. When the trigger is pulled, it activates the hammer (or the internal firing mechanism) which, when released, causes the firing pin to strike and fire the cartridge.

When a semi-automatic is fired, the *slide* moves to the rear, ejecting the empty cartridge case and usually cocking the pistol in the process. The cartridges located in the magazine are forced upward by the *magazine spring* into the path of the slide. When the slide (under pressure from a *recoil spring* or *slide spring* to return to a closed position) moves forward, it picks up and pushes the top cartridge into the chamber.

There are three different types of semi-automatic actions: *single-action*, *double-action*, and *double-action-only*. As with the revolver, these actions describe the function of the trigger in relation to the operation of the pistol.

In a *single-action* semi-automatic, the trigger performs a single task—releasing the hammer or the internal firing mechanism so that the firing pin hits the cartridge.

In a *double-action* semi-automatic, the trigger performs two tasks.

It cocks the hammer or internal firing mechanism for the first shot, and also releases the hammer or the internal firing mechanism. After the first shot is fired, the movement of the slide will cock the hammer or internal firing mechanism for all successive shots, and the trigger will be used only to release the hammer or internal firing mechanism.

In a *double-action-only* semi-automatic, the trigger will cock and release the hammer or internal firing mechanism on the first shot and all successive shots. The slide will chamber a new cartridge after each shot, as it does for the other types of semi-automatic actions, but it will *not* cock the hammer or internal firing mechanism. The cock-and-release action is accomplished by pulling the trigger for each shot. In this way, the action of the trigger is similar to that of a double-action revolver. However, in most double-action-only semi-automatics, the hammer cannot be manually cocked to a single-action position as it can in a double-action revolver.

Remember that some semi-automatic pistols may vary from the above descriptions due to the large variety of mechanical designs available today. Always be sure to carefully read and understand the instruction manual for a pistol. And if questions still exist, be sure to consult a knowledgeable person.

CHAPTER 1 REVIEW

1. The two most common types of pistols are the _Revolvers_
   and the _Semi automatics_

2. The three major components contained in both of the above pistols
   are the _action_, the _frame_, and the
   Barrel.

3. The _action_ is a group of moving parts used to load,
   fire, and unload a pistol.

4. What is the difference between a single-action revolver and a
   double-action revolver?
   Single action - trigger releases the hammer
   DBL action - trigger cocks the gun & releases
   the hammer

5. Where are the chambers located on a revolver?
   multiple chambers in the
   cylinder

6. Where is the chamber located on a semi-automatic pistol?
   On the Barrel

7. Describe the actions in the following types of semi-automatics:
   single-action, double-action, and double-action-only.
   Single action - trigger releases the hammer or
   internal firing mechanism
   Double - trigger cocks the gun & releases the
   hammer

8

   DBL only - trigger cocks the gun, releases
   the hammer for the 1st shot & all successive shots

N O T E S

CHAPTER 2

CARTRIDGE PARTS

A pistol cartridge is made up of four basic components: the *case*, the *primer*, the *powder charge*, and the *bullet*.

The *case* is a metal cylinder (usually made of brass) that is closed at one end and contains the other three components.

The *primer* is an impact-sensitive chemical compound used for ignition. In a rimfire cartridge, it is contained in the inside rim of the case's base. In a center-fire cartridge, the primer is contained in a small metal cup, and is located in the center of the case's base.

The *powder charge* is a fast-burning chemical compound used as a propellant, and is contained inside the body of the case.

The *bullet* is a projectile, usually made of lead and sometimes covered with a layer of copper or other metal, and is located at the mouth of the case.

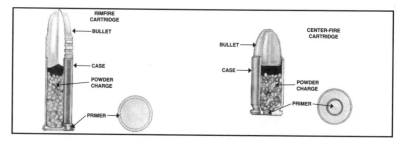

A cartridge is also commonly referred to as a *round*. A *live round* is a cartridge that contains a primer, a powder charge, and a bullet. A *dummy round* contains a bullet, but does not contain a primer or a powder charge, and therefore cannot be fired.

TYPES OF CARTRIDGES

The two types of modern pistol cartridges are *rimfire* and *center-fire*. The names for both types of cartridges are derived from the location of the primer.

CARTRIDGE FIRING SEQUENCE

Pulling the trigger of a pistol will cause the firing pin to hit and ignite the primer. The flame generated by the primer in turn ignites the powder in the cartridge. The powder burns very rapidly and produces a high volume of gas. These expanding gases push the bullet out of the cartridge case and propel it out of the pistol barrel at a high rate of speed.

USING THE PROPER CARTRIDGE

It is essential to always use the proper cartridge in a pistol. Only a cartridge that has been designed for a particular gun can be fired safely in that gun. It is dangerous to fire the wrong cartridge in a pistol.

Even though a cartridge may appear to fit in a chamber or magazine, it may not actually be the correct cartridge for that pistol. As a basic safety measure, proper identification of cartridges is mandatory.

To ensure the use of the correct cartridge, the pistol must first be examined to determine the cartridge that it is designed to fire. This cartridge designation will be marked on the barrel, frame, or slide.

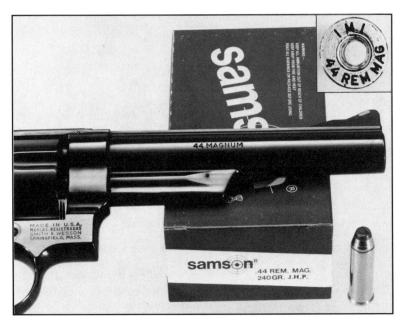

Next, examine and identify the cartridges. Most center-fire cartridges have the cartridge designation stamped on the base of the cartridge case around the primer. This marking is known as the *headstamp*. (Rimfire cartridges will not have a designation headstamp.) Cartridge designations are also marked on the factory box or carton containing the cartridges.

Some cartridges will have a +P (*Plus P*) or +P+ (*Plus P Plus*) designation. These cartridges are loaded to higher pressures than standard ammunition. The original boxes containing cartridges loaded to +P or +P+ pressures are marked with this designation, and the cartridges may sometimes be stamped +P or +P+ on the bases of the cartridge cases. These higher pressure cartridges should only be fired in guns that are designed for such use.

Be sure to check the pistol instruction manual for guidelines concerning proper cartridge use.

Finally, compare the cartridge designations with the cartridge information marked on the pistol. Be sure all the various designations are the same.

If it is not clear whether a gun is approved for +P or +P+ cartridges, or if questions still exist about the correct cartridge to use in a pistol, consult the gun manufacturer or a knowledgeable individual. Don't gamble with safety!

On the following pages is an illustrated listing of the most popular pistol cartridges.

POPULAR PISTOL CARTRIDGES

RIMFIRE CARTRIDGES

.22 Long Rifle—One of the most popular cartridges made for pistols and rifles. Because of its low recoil, noise, and cost, it is an excellent cartridge to use when learning how to shoot. Probably the most popular match cartridge in existence, it can also be used to hunt small game.

.22 Winchester Magnum—Introduced in 1959 by Winchester, it is an elongated and powerful .22 rimfire cartridge. It can be used for hunting small game.

CENTER-FIRE CARTRIDGES

.25 ACP—Known in Europe as the 6.35mm Browning, this cartridge was introduced in 1902 in conjunction with a small Colt semi-automatic pistol. It is the smallest commonly produced center-fire pistol cartridge. Many small pocket pistols are chambered for the .25 ACP.

.32 ACP—Commonly known in Europe as the 7.65 mm Browning, this cartridge was introduced about 1899 for use in the Browning-designed autoloading pocket pistol manufactured by Fabrique Nationale in Belgium. This cartridge is used mainly in small pocket pistols.

.380 ACP—Also known as the .380 Auto, 9mm Browning Short, 9mm Kurz, and 9mm Corto. Introduced about 1912 for a Browning-designed autoloading pistol manufactured by Fabrique Nationale in Belgium. Although used in many small semi-automatic pistols, this cartridge also has many large semi-automatic models chambered for it, and has been used by uniformed police in Europe.

9mm Luger (Parabellum)—This cartridge was introduced in 1902 for the Luger pistol. The 9mm Luger/Parabellum is one of the most popular pistol cartridges used today. It is used by the U.S. military and by NATO allies.

.38 Super Colt Automatic—Introduced in 1929 by Colt, the .38 Super is a more powerful version of the .38 ACP cartridge. Dimensionally the same as the .38 ACP but loaded to higher pressures, the .38 Super should not be fired in guns intended only for .38 ACP cartridges.

.38 Special—Introduced by Smith & Wesson about 1902. One of the most popular revolver cartridges made. Police officers around the country have traditionally carried .38 Special revolvers. This cartridge is available in standard pressure loadings, and in +P and +P+ loadings. However, before using +P or +P+ cartridges in a pistol, be sure that it is approved for such use.

.357 Magnum—Introduced by Smith & Wesson in 1935. More powerful than the .38 Special, the .357 Magnum is based on the .38 Special cartridge case lengthened by about ⅒th of an inch.

10mm Auto—Designed in the early 1980s for the Dornaus and Dixon Bren Ten pistol, the 10mm Auto cartridge has gained in popularity. Today, a number of manufacturers make pistols that are chambered for it. More powerful than the .357 Magnum, the 10mm Auto cartridge brings magnum power to average-sized semi-automatic pistols.

.40 S&W—Introduced commercially about 1990 for use in semi-automatic pistols. The .40 S&W is a shorter version of the 10mm Auto cartridge, and produces less recoil and muzzle blast. However, for self-defense purposes, the cartridge still has very good stopping power.

.41 Magnum—Introduced by Remington in 1964 for the Smith & Wesson Model 57 revolver. The .41 Magnum was intended to provide an intermediate-powered cartridge between the .357 Magnum and the .44 Magnum. However, the .41 Magnum has not achieved the popularity of those cartridges.

.44 Special—Introduced in 1907 by Smith & Wesson, this cartridge was designed to be more powerful than the .44 S&W Russian cartridge (which was originally loaded with blackpowder).

.44 Magnum—Introduced by Remington for Smith & Wesson in 1956. This cartridge was the most powerful standard handgun cartridge at that time. It is used in hunting medium size game at close ranges.

.45 ACP—Developed by John Browning in 1905, and adopted as the U.S. military pistol cartridge from 1911 to the late 1980s. This cartridge is currently used in conventional and other types of pistol shooting competitions.

.45 Colt—Also known as the .45 Long Colt. Introduced in 1873 as a blackpowder cartridge for the famous Colt *Peacemaker* single-action revolver. Today, the .45 Colt is loaded with modern smokeless powder by many ammunition companies, and a number of gun manufacturers currently produce revolvers that are chambered for this powerful cartridge. (Early-model Colt revolvers with serial numbers 160,000 and below were made during the era of black powder. Such revolvers should not be fired with smokeless powder ammunition.)

CARE AND STORAGE OF AMMUNITION

Always keep ammunition in the factory box or carton. The labeling on the original container will help to identify the cartridges so that they can be used in the pistol for which they are intended. In order to help ensure that the cartridges will function properly, store them in an area where there are not unusual variations of temperature and humidity. Extreme high temperatures, such as those found in an attic or car trunk, should be avoided. A cool, dry area is best for storage purposes. For safety reasons, ammunition should be stored separately from guns. Also be certain to store ammunition so that it is not accessible to unauthorized persons, especially children.

Always wipe fingerprints from ammunition. Acids, salts, and other chemicals contained in fingerprints can cause corrosion. Also beware of storing cartridges in leather cartridge belts—acids in the leather can cause corrosion.

Cartridges should never be submerged in water or be exposed to any solvents, petroleum products (including gun oil), bore cleaner, ammonia, or other chemicals. These materials can penetrate a cartridge and cause the primer or the powder to deteriorate. This type of damage to a cartridge can result in the following malfunctions:

Misfire—a *failure* of the cartridge to fire after the primer has been struck by the firing pin.

Hangfire—a *perceptible delay* in the ignition of a cartridge after the primer has been struck by the firing pin.

Squib load—development of less than normal pressure or velocity after ignition of the cartridge.

When a cartridge fails to fire immediately, it will not be known at first whether the problem is a *misfire* or a *hangfire*. Keep the pistol pointed in a safe direction—a hangfire condition might exist and the cartridge could still fire. Don't attempt to open the action of the pistol to remove the cartridge for at least 30 seconds.

If anything unusual is noticed when a shot is fired, such as a difference in recoil or noise, stop firing immediately. A *squib load* may have been fired. Keep the muzzle pointed in a safe direction and unload the gun as explained in Chapter 4 of this book. *Check to be sure that the chamber is empty.* Then, with the action open, carefully run a cleaning rod through the barrel to be sure that it is not obstructed. (Squib loads can result in the bullet failing to exit the barrel. If the bullet is lodged in the barrel, the firing of another shot could cause serious injury or damage.)

C H A P T E R   2   R E V I E W

1. The four basic components of a pistol cartridge are the
   _Case_____ , the _Bullet_____ , the
   _Primer_____ , and the _Powder_____ .

2. The basic difference between a rimfire cartridge and a center-fire
   cartridge is the location of the _Primer_____

3. Describe the ways to determine the proper cartridge for a pistol.
   Cartridge is marked on pistol
   Read the manual
   compare cartidge designatias w/ the
   pistol - ex Amine markings on Center fire
   cartridges
4. Describe the proper ways to store ammunition.
   Cool + dry, in original Box
   No extremes in temperature
   Safe from unauthorized persons
   away from the firearm
5. Define the following:

   a. Misfire.- primer fails to ignight

   b. Hangfire. delay in ignition

   c. Squib load.
      low velocity fire -
      Round may remain in the
      gun Barrel -

19

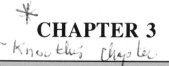

CHAPTER 3

~ Know this chapter

USING A PISTOL SAFELY

Safety must be the first concern when handling or using a pistol or any other type of firearm. The need for caution exists wherever guns are located—at home, on the shooting range, or in the field.

WHAT CAUSES GUN ACCIDENTS?

Most gun accidents are caused by _ignorance_ and/or _carelessness_. Ignorance is a lack of knowledge—a person who handles a gun without knowing the gun safety rules or how to operate the gun is exhibiting a dangerous lack of knowledge. Equally dangerous is the person who, although knowing the gun safety rules and how to properly operate a gun, becomes careless in properly applying this knowledge. In both of these cases, accidents can easily happen. But when people practice responsible ownership and use of guns, accidents _don't_ happen.

THE THREE FUNDAMENTAL GUN SAFETY RULES

The three fundamental rules of gun safety must always be applied simultaneously when handling or using a gun:

1. Always keep the gun pointed in a safe direction.
2. Always keep your finger off the trigger until ready to shoot.
3. Always keep the gun unloaded until ready to use.

These three rules are so important that each one should be discussed in more detail:

1. _Always keep the gun pointed in a safe direction_—This rule means that a gun must always be pointed so that even if it were unintentionally discharged, it would not cause injury or damage. The key to observing this rule is to always control where the muzzle (the front end of the gun barrel) is pointing.

   Common sense will dictate the safest direction; this direction can vary depending upon circumstances. For example, when outside, it is usually safe to point the gun up or down. When inside a building, however, additional judgment and care must be exercised. If on the bottom floor, don't point the gun up—a shot could go through the ceiling to a room above. If upstairs, don't point the gun down—a shot might penetrate the floor.

Regardless of location, always be aware of where the gun is pointing and of what might lie beyond the immediate view of the area. And, of course, *never* point a gun at another person!

2. *Always keep your finger off the trigger until ready to shoot*—When holding a gun, a person has a natural tendency to place the index finger on the trigger. *Don't do it!* Instead, while pointing the gun in a safe direction, rest your finger along the side of the gun. Never touch the trigger until actually ready to fire the gun.

3. *Always keep the gun unloaded until ready to use*—Whenever picking up a gun, keep it pointed in a safe direction, keep your finger off the trigger, and immediately open the action and look into the chamber to be sure that it is empty. (In semi-automatic pistols, the chamber is located at the rear of the barrel. Revolvers have multiple chambers which are located in the cylinder.)

If the gun has a detachable magazine, remove it *before* opening the action. If the magazine is not detachable, be sure to remove the cartridges from it. Remember, always keep the gun pointed in a safe direction and keep your finger off the trigger.

If uncertain how to open the action and unload a gun, leave it alone and get help from a knowledgeable person.

As a general rule, a gun stored for any purpose other than personal protection should never be kept loaded in the home. Only in unusual circumstances should a loaded gun be kept in the home, and then only if special care and precautions are taken. For example, a gun kept in the home for protection is essentially always in use; however, the gun must be stored in a secure place where it is totally inaccessible to all unauthorized users (both children and adults). And, of course, all local laws must be observed.

Finally, treat every gun as if it were loaded. Even in those instances when a gun is *known* to be unloaded, continue to treat it as if it were loaded.

OTHER SAFETY RULES

The following gun safety rules should also be observed when using or storing a gun:

1. *Be sure the gun is safe to operate.* Just like other tools, guns need regular maintenance to remain operable. Regular cleaning and proper storage are a part of the gun's general upkeep. If there is any question concerning a gun's condition, a knowledgeable gunsmith should look at it.

2. *Know how to use the gun safely.* Before handling a gun, learn how it operates. Know its basic parts, how to safely open and close the action, and how to remove ammunition from chambers and/or magazines.

   Nothing can ever replace safe gun handling. Don't rely on a gun's safety mechanism. Like any mechanical device, it can fail. Use it, but don't let it be a substitute for safe gun handling and observance of the three fundamental rules of gun safety. A defective mechanism could result in an accident.

   Never pull the trigger on a gun when the safety is in the "ON" position, or when the safety is located anywhere between the "ON" and the "OFF" positions. If the safety mechanism is defective, the gun could fire without any trigger contact when the safety is moved to the "OFF" position at a later time.

   Dont't play with the safety by changing its position constantly . . . leave the safety in the "ON" position until absolutely ready to fire.

3. *Use only the correct ammunition for the gun.* Only BBs, pellets, cartridges, or shells designed for a particular gun can be fired safely in that gun. Most guns have the ammunition type stamped on the barrel. Ammunition can be identified by information printed on the box and sometimes stamped on the cartridge. Do not shoot the gun unless the proper ammunition is used.

4. *Know the target and what is beyond.* Be absolutely sure that the target has been identified beyond any doubt. Equally important, be aware of the area beyond the target. This means observing the prospective area of fire before shooting. Never fire in a direction in which there are people or any other potential

for mishap. When practicing, be sure that there is a safe backstop. Always think first. Shoot second.

5. *Wear eye and ear protection as appropriate.* Gunshots are loud and the noise can cause hearing damage. Guns can also emit debris and hot gas that could cause eye injury. For these reasons, safety glasses and ear protection are *strongly* recommended.

6. *Never use alcohol or drugs before or while shooting.* Alcohol, as well as any other substance likely to impair normal mental or physical bodily functions, must not be used before or while handling or shooting guns.

Remember that even over-the-counter (non-prescription) medications can impair judgment and cause undesirable physical side effects, such as loss of coordination, vision difficulties, tremors, and drowsiness, which could contribute to an accident.

7. *Store guns so they are not accessible to unauthorized persons.* Many factors must be considered when deciding where and how to store guns. A person's particular situation will be a major part of the consideration. Remember that safe and secure storage requires that unauthorized individuals (especially children) be denied access to guns.

Dozens of gun storage devices are available on the market today: gun cabinets, gun safes, wall racks, hard and soft gun cases, strongboxes, etc. In addition, various types of locking devices which attach directly to the gun, such as trigger locks, are available. However, these mechanical locking devices, just like the mechanical safeties built into guns, can fail and should not be used as a substitute for safe gun handling and the observance of all gun safety rules.

Ammunition, as a general rule, should be stored separately from guns. It is preferable to keep the ammunition in the manufacturers' original boxes. Ammunition should be stored in a cool, dry area and in a manner so that it is not accessible to unauthorized persons.

8. *Be aware that certain types of guns and many shooting activities require additional safety precautions.*

OTHER SAFETY SUGGESTIONS

- Be a knowledgeable gun handler and user. Read the instruction manual for the gun carefully, and understand it thoroughly before attempting to use, load or unload, disassemble or assemble, or clean the gun. If any questions or problems exist, don't guess or experiment! Consult a knowledgeable individual for assistance. Also become familiar with various publications which may increase gun knowledge and skills. (See Appendix F for a listing of helpful NRA publications.)

- Before starting to clean a gun, be certain that it is not loaded. *Check to be sure that the chamber is empty.* As an additional safety measure, never allow ammunition to be present while cleaning guns.

- Cleaning a gun also provides an opportunity to check the proper functioning of the gun. If a problem is discovered, don't try to fix it; take it to a competent gunsmith, or return it to the manufacturer for repair.

- Always be sure that the gun barrel is free from obstructions. A cleaning patch or the wrong size ammunition could obstruct the barrel. If the gun is dropped, the barrel could become obstructed with mud, snow, or other foreign matter. Before checking the barrel, be sure to keep the muzzle pointed in a safe direction, keep your finger off the trigger, and unload the gun as explained in Chapter 4 of this book. *Check to be sure that the chamber is empty.* Then, with the action open, visually inspect the barrel to be sure that it is not obstructed.

- When handing a pistol to another person, always be sure that the muzzle is pointed in a safe direction, your finger is off the trigger, the action is open, the magazine (if any) has been removed, and all chambers are empty.

- Carry only one type of ammunition to avoid mixing different types.

- If in possession of an old or antique firearm, or a gun that is a military souvenir, be sure that it is unloaded. If uncertain how to determine this, consult a knowledgeable person for assistance.

- Never fire at surfaces that can cause a bullet to ricochet, such as water or hard, flat objects.
- Know the maximum range of the ammunition being used. Consider the consequences of the shot if the bullet should miss its target or ricochet.
- Never rush a shot—take time to make sure that all safety rules are being observed. If there isn't time to do this, then don't shoot! Remember that once a shot has been fired, it's too late to change things—the bullet can't be called back and its direction can't be altered.
- If a cartridge fails to fire when the trigger is pulled, keep the gun pointed in a safe direction. Because the cartridge might still fire, don't attempt to open the action of the gun to remove the cartridge for at least 30 seconds.
- If anything unusual is noticed when a shot is fired, such as a difference in recoil or in noise, stop firing immediately. Keep the muzzle pointed in a safe direction, keep your finger off the trigger, and unload the gun as explained in Chapter 4 of this book. *Check to be sure that the chamber is empty.* Then, with the action open, visually inspect the barrel to be sure that it is not obstructed. (A defective cartridge which develops less than standard pressure or velocity could result in the bullet failing to exit the barrel. If the bullet is lodged in the barrel, the firing of another shot could cause serious injury or damage.)
- Don't bypass the magazine of a semi-automatic pistol by manually inserting a round directly into the chamber. If the cartridge is not seated properly in the chamber, it is possible for the slide to hit and ignite the primer when the slide returns to its forward position.
- Beware of fatigue—it can cause persons to become careless, clumsy, and inattentive. If signs of fatigue appear, stop all shooting activities.
- Always comply with all regulations at club and public ranges.
- Always comply with all federal, state, and local firearm laws.

SPECIAL RESPONSIBILITIES FOR PARENTS

Parents should be aware that a child could discover a gun when a responsible adult is not present. This situation could occur in the child's own home, the home of a neighbor, friend, or relative, or in a public place (such as a park). To avoid the possibility of an accident in such a situation, the child should be taught to apply the following gun safety rules:

These four rules are part of a special accident-prevention program known as the Eddie Eagle® Gun Safety Program. Developed by the NRA for young children (pre-kindergarten through sixth grade), it uses the friendly character of Eddie Eagle to teach children to follow Eddie's four rules.

RANGE SAFETY

A properly supervised pistol range is one of the safest places to enjoy shooting. The operators of most ranges use standard range commands to control the shooting and to promote uniform safe practices.

The person in charge of the range is known as the *range officer.* The range officer's primary duties are to control all shooting activities on the range and to ensure that the shooters are obeying all safety rules. The range officer will issue spoken orders known as *range commands.* The purpose of these range commands is to provide clear, concise, and standardized instructions to all shooters. These commands must be obeyed by all shooters.

Each shooter is responsible for knowing, understanding, and obeying all of the commands spoken by the range officer. A few of the commands commonly used are *LOAD, COMMENCE FIRING,* and *CEASE FIRING.*

LOAD—When shooters are on the firing line and this command is given by the range officer, the pistol may be loaded. (Prior to receiving this command, the shooter must be sure that the pistol is unloaded, the muzzle is pointed in a safe direction, and the action is open.)

COMMENCE FIRING—This command by the range officer means that firing may begin as soon as the shooters are ready. (The range officer may also signal "COMMENCE FIRING" by moving the targets into view.) *All* shooters should be wearing hearing protectors and safety glasses for protection against gun noise and debris.

CEASE FIRING—This command means to stop shooting *immediately.* Even a shooter who is in the process of pulling the trigger for a shot must immediately stop, remove his or her finger from the trigger, and, while keeping the muzzle pointed in a safe direction, wait for further instructions from the range officer.

The "CEASE FIRING" command can be used during normal range procedures or in an emergency situation.

An example of a normal range procedure would be the range officer's use of "CEASE FIRING" when time expires in a formal pistol match. Upon hearing this command, a competitor should immediately cease firing, take his or her finger off the trigger, point the gun in a safe direction, and await further instructions from the range officer. These instructions could include such commands as "UNLOAD . . . CYLINDERS OPEN . . . MAGAZINES OUT . . . SLIDES BACK . . . GUNS ON THE BENCH."

In an emergency situation, the "CEASE FIRING" command is not restricted to use by the range officer, but should be used by *anyone* who detects an unsafe situation. If an unsafe situation occurs, don't wait for the range officer's intervention—*call out* "CEASE FIRING" immediately!

The range officer can also signal "CEASE FIRING" by a short, sharp blast on a whistle or by moving the targets out of view.

Additional commands may be used by the range officer depending upon the shooting facility, the number of persons shooting, and other variables. These additional commands are generally used to direct the flow of shooters to and from the firing line and to provide necessary instructions or information.

CHAPTER 3 REVIEW

1. Most gun accidents are caused by _Ignorance_ and _carelessness_.

2. The three fundamental gun safety rules are:

   a. _Point the firearm in a safe direction_.

   b. _don't load until ready to fire_.

   c. _Keep your finger off the trigger_.

3. A shooter should always "know the target and _beyond the target_."

4. Should a gun's safety mechanism be relied upon?
   _____ Yes   _X_ No
   Explain the reasons for selecting the above answer:
   Safetys are mechanical & can fail

5. Why should safety glasses and hearing protection be worn when shooting?

   Firearm emits gases & airborne particle that can damage eyes -
   Loud report can damage hearing

6. Three commonly used range commands are:

   a. Cease fire .

   b. load .

   c. Commence fire .

7. Guns should be stored so that they are not accessible to

   unauthorized people .

8. Who may call out the "CEASE FIRING" command on a range?

   anyone

N O T E S

CHAPTER 4

OPERATING A PISTOL

Loading, preparing to fire, and unloading a pistol are basic exercises that the pistol shooter must master. This chapter will present the basic guidelines for performing these operations for most revolvers and semi-automatic pistols. However, because there are many different types of pistols on the market and because operating procedures vary from model to model, the instruction manual for the pistol should be read and understood before operating it. If any questions still exist after reading the manual, seek the advice of a knowledgeable person.

The guidelines listed in this section of the book are for a right-handed person; left-handed persons should make appropriate adjustments to these guidelines.

REVOLVER OPERATION

SINGLE-ACTION REVOLVERS

1. To Load:

    a. Keeping the gun pointed in a safe direction and the index finger off the trigger, hold the pistol in the left hand with the muzzle pointed downward.

    b. Use the right thumb on the spur of the hammer to pull the hammer back one or two clicks. (See Figure 1.)

Figure 1

This action will release the cylinder so that it can be rotated. (With some models, the hammer will not have to be pulled back; the cylinder will be released by opening the loading gate—see the next step immediately below.)

c. With the right thumb, open the loading gate. (See Figure 2.)

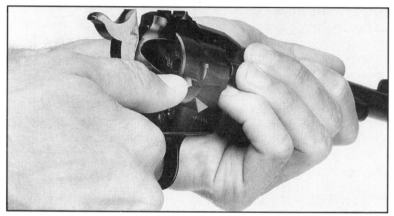

Figure 2

d. Align an empty chamber with the loading port by turning the cylinder with the fingers of the left hand.

e. With the right hand, insert a cartridge into the chamber. (See Figure 3.)

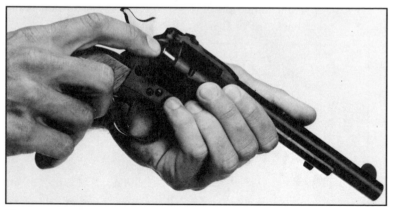

Figure 3

f. With the left hand, rotate the cylinder to the next empty chamber; insert another cartridge with the right hand.

g. When finished loading, close the loading gate with the right hand.

2. To Cock:

a. Keeping the gun pointed in a safe direction and with the index finger off the trigger, grip the gun with the right hand.

b. Using the left thumb on the spur of the hammer, pull the hammer all the way to the rear until it locks in place. (See Figure 4.)

Figure 4

3. To Uncock:

a. Keeping the gun pointed in a safe direction and with the index finger off the trigger, place the left thumb between the hammer and the frame.

b. Place the right thumb firmly on the spur of the cocked hammer.

c. While controlling the hammer with the right thumb, pull the trigger with the right index finger to release the hammer; use the right thumb to lower the hammer gently against the left thumb. (See Figure 5.)

d. Continuing to pull the trigger with the right index finger and maintaining control of the hammer with the right thumb, carefully remove the left thumb from under the hammer, and use the right thumb to slowly lower the hammer completely.

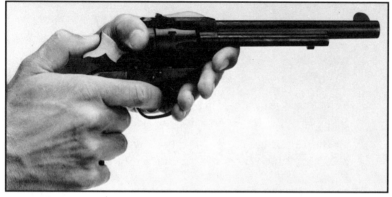

Figure 5

e. Remove the index finger from the trigger. With the left thumb on the spur of the hammer, pull the hammer back one click to its safety position.

4. To Unload:

a. Keeping the gun pointed in a safe direction and the index finger off the trigger, hold the pistol in the left hand with the muzzle pointed downward.

b. Use the right thumb on the spur of the hammer to pull the hammer back one or two clicks. This action will release the cylinder so that it can be rotated. (As mentioned previously, the hammer will not have to be pulled back on some models; the cylinder will be released by opening the loading gate.)

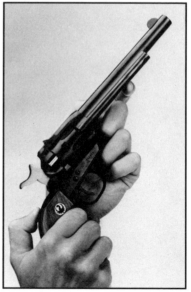

c. With the right thumb, open the loading gate.

d. Align a loaded chamber with the loading port by turning the cylinder with the fingers of the left hand.

Figure 6

e. Elevate the muzzle in a safe direction. With the left hand, use the ejector rod to push the loaded cartridge (or empty cartridge case) out of the chamber. (See Figure 6.) Continue this process until all chambers are empty.

f. Rotate the cylinder with the left hand while visually checking the chambers to be sure that all cartridges have been removed.

g. Close the loading gate with the right hand.

h. Keeping the pistol pointed in a safe direction, place the right thumb firmly on the spur of the hammer. While controlling the hammer with the right thumb, pull the trigger with the right index finger to release the hammer; use the right thumb to gently lower the hammer completely. (See Figure 7.)

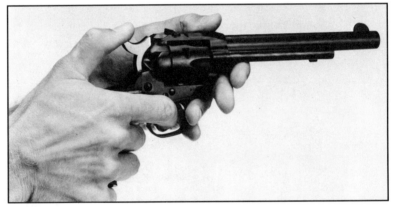

Figure 7

DOUBLE-ACTION REVOLVERS

1. To Load:

a. Keeping the gun pointed in a safe direction and with the index finger off the trigger, use the right hand to place the pistol in the palm of the left hand.

b. Release the cylinder latch with the right thumb, and push the cylinder out with the two middle fingers of the left hand. (See Figure 8.)

Figure 8

c. Continuing to hold the pistol in the left hand, point the muzzle in a safe direction and use the right hand to load the cartridges into the chambers of the cylinder. (See Figure 9.)

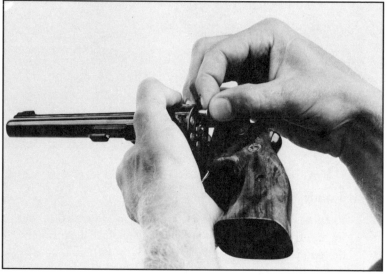

Figure 9

d. Regrip the pistol with the right hand, and use the left thumb to push the cylinder closed.

2. To Cock:

   a. Keeping the gun pointed in a safe direction and with the index finger off the trigger, grip the gun with the right hand.

   b. Using the left thumb on the spur of the hammer, pull the hammer all the way to the rear until it locks in place. (See Figure 10.)

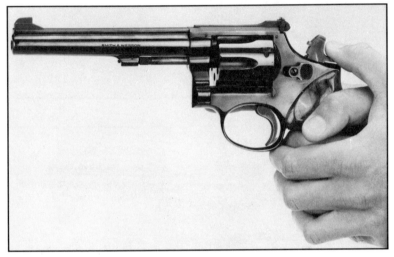

Figure 10

3. To Uncock:

   a. Keeping the gun pointed in a safe direction and with the index finger off the trigger, place the left thumb between the hammer and the frame. (See Figure 11.)

   b. Place the right thumb firmly on the spur of the cocked hammer.

   c. While controlling the hammer with the right thumb, pull the trigger with the right index finger to release the hammer; use the right thumb to lower the hammer gently against the left thumb. (See Figure 12.)

   d. *Remove the index finger from the trigger.*

   e. While continuing to control the hammer with the right thumb, carefully remove the left thumb from under the hammer, and use the right thumb to slowly lower the hammer completely.

Figure 11

Figure 12

4. To Unload:

a. Keeping the gun pointed in a safe direction and with the index finger off the trigger, use the right hand to place the pistol in the palm of the left hand.

b. Release the cylinder latch with the right thumb, and push the cylinder out with the two middle fingers of the left hand. (See Figure 13.)

c. Place the left thumb on the ejector rod.

d. Elevate the muzzle in a safe direction. Use the left thumb to firmly push the ejector rod completely to the rear; the loaded cartridges (or empty cartridge cases) will be pushed out of the chambers by the action of the ejector rod. Use the right hand to catch the ejected cartridges. (See Figure 14.)

e. Inspect the chambers to be sure that they are empty.

f. Gently close the empty cylinder. (Never roughly open or close the cylinder.)

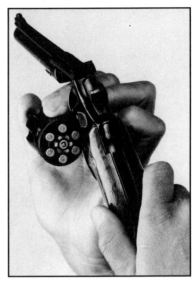

Figure 13

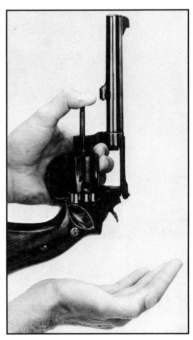

Figure 14

SEMI-AUTOMATIC PISTOL OPERATION

TO LOAD:

1. Keeping the gun pointed in a safe direction and the index finger off the trigger, hold the pistol in the right hand.

2. Inspect the pistol to be sure that the magazine has been removed. (If the magazine is still in the pistol, remove it by activating the magazine release with the left hand.)

3. Use the left hand to move the slide to the rear. (See Figure 15.) If the pistol has a slide stop, use it to keep the slide open. (See Figure 16.)

Figure 15

Figure 16

42

4. Inspect the chamber to be sure that it is empty.

5. Lay the pistol down with the muzzle pointing in a safe direction.

6. Hold the magazine in either hand, and load it by pushing the cartridges down into and toward the rear of the magazine. (See Figure 17.) When finished, lay the magazine down in a secure place.

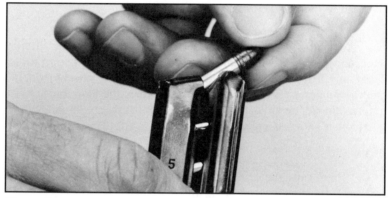

Figure 17

7. Pick up the pistol with the right hand, being sure to keep the pistol pointed in a safe direction and the index finger off the trigger.

8. With the left hand, insert the loaded magazine into the pistol. (See Figure 18.)

Figure 18

9. With the left hand, release the slide stop so that the slide will move forward, stripping off the first cartridge from the top of the magazine and loading it into the chamber. If the pistol does not have a slide stop, grasp the rear portion of the slide with the left hand, move the slide completely to the rear, and then release the slide so that it can move forward.

10. The pistol is now loaded and ready to fire.

TO UNCOCK:

As mentioned earlier, because of the large number of different mechanical designs, semi-automatic pistols vary greatly in operation. The many different methods of uncocking all of these various models are too numerous to describe here. Therefore, the best source of information for detailed instructions is the instruction manual for the pistol or a knowledgeable person.

TO UNLOAD:

1. Keeping the gun pointed in a safe direction and the index finger off the trigger, hold the pistol in the right hand.

2. Push the magazine release, and remove the magazine from the pistol.

3. Grasp the rear portion of the slide with the left hand and move the slide completely to the rear, ejecting the cartridge from the chamber.

4. Visually and physically inspect the chamber to be sure that it is empty.

C H A P T E R   4   R E V I E W

1. Briefly describe the unloading procedure for:
   Keep firearm pointed in safe direction
   a. Single-action revolvers.

   b. Double-action revolvers.

   c. Semi-automatics.
   Remove the magazine
   expose the Chamber by pulling
   the slide remove the round
   lock the slide open

2. If a person is uncertain as to how a pistol operates, what are the two things that he or she should do?

   a. _Read the manual_____ .

   _____ .

   b. _Seek the advice of an_____
   _authorized person_____ .

CHAPTER 5

CLEANING, STORING, AND TRANSPORTING A PISTOL

A pistol is a valuable piece of precision equipment. It must be given proper care if it is to operate correctly and safely. Taking proper care of a pistol will also maintain its value and extend its life.

WHEN TO CLEAN

A pistol should be cleaned every time that it is used. Regular cleaning is needed to ensure that a pistol will operate properly and reliably. Cleaning also preserves the finish of a pistol and protects against rust.

If a pistol is stored for a long period of time, it should be carefully cleaned before it is fired. Dirt and moisture can accumulate in the pistol and may cause it to malfunction.

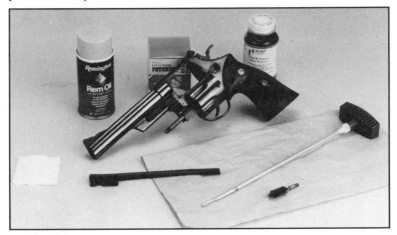

CLEANING MATERIALS REQUIRED

The following basic materials are needed to clean a pistol:

- Cloth patches
- Cleaning rod
- Soft cloth

- Cleaning rod attachments (which are screwed onto the end of the cleaning rod):
  - Bore brush (Bristles are usually metal.)
  - Tips to hold cloth patches
- Small brush (An old, clean toothbrush is good for this purpose.)
- Bore cleaner (a special liquid solvent for gun bores)
- Gun oil

Cleaning rods, rod attachments, and patches are sold in various sizes to fit the different calibers of pistols. Be sure to use the proper size for the pistol.

CLEANING GUIDELINES

IMPORTANT!! Before starting to clean a pistol, *be absolutely certain* that it is unloaded and the action is open. No ammunition should be present while cleaning a pistol.

1. Attach the bore brush to the cleaning rod and dip the brush in bore cleaner.

2. Run the brush through the bore of the pistol barrel 8–10 times. Clean from the rear of the barrel whenever possible to reduce muzzle wear. Be sure that the brush emerges from the barrel completely before drawing it back through the barrel. Also be careful not to damage the muzzle of the barrel during this cleaning process. (See Figure 19.)

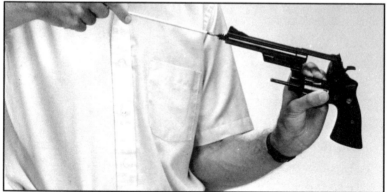

Figure 19

3. Remove the bore brush from the cleaning rod and attach a patch-holder tip. Attach a cloth patch to the tip. Dip the cloth patch in bore cleaner and run it through the bore several times. (See Figure 20.) Remove the cloth patch from the rod tip.

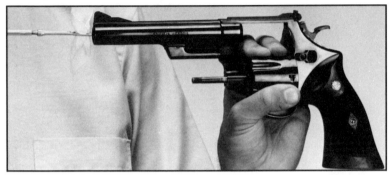

Figure 20

4. Attach a clean, dry patch to the rod tip and run it through the bore several times.

5. Inspect the dry patch. If the patch is dirty, repeat Steps 1 through 4 above until the dry patch comes out clean.

6. When satisfied with the appearance of the dry patch, run a lightly-oiled patch through the bore.

7. If cleaning a revolver, repeat Steps 1 through 6 above for each of the chambers in the cylinder. (See Figure 21.)

   Also use a small brush to thoroughly clean the extractor and the area around it, including the underside of the extractor and the rear face of the cylinder. (See Figure 22.) Be sure

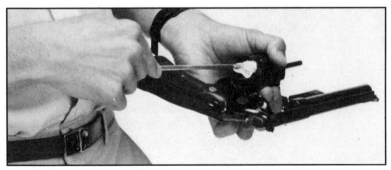

Figure 21

that dirt, powder particles, and other debris are not left under the extractor. Also clean the front face of the cylinder.

Figure 22

8. Wipe the outside of the pistol with a clean cloth and a light coat of gun oil. (See Figure 23.) After the pistol has been cleaned for storage, avoid any skin contact with the metal parts. Chemicals in skin oil and in perspiration can cause rust.

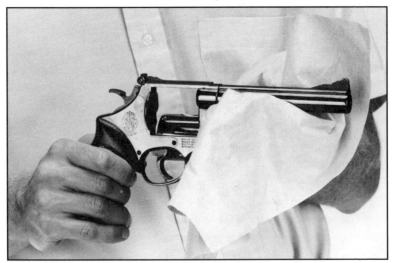
Figure 23

STORING A PISTOL

As mentioned in Chapter 3 of this book, a variety of storage devices, such as gun cabinets, gun safes, hard and soft cases, and strongboxes, are available for a pistol. However, the most important thing to remember and practice when it comes to gun storage is to *store guns so they are not accessible to unauthorized persons*. This gun safety rule cannot be emphasized too strongly.

TRANSPORTING A PISTOL

The transporting of a pistol is governed by a myriad of federal, state, and local laws. These laws may differ from one locality to another, and may conflict with each other.

The following information should not be considered as legal advice or as a restatement of applicable laws. Always consult a competent attorney concerning any legal questions regarding a pistol.

TRANSPORTING WITHIN A STATE

In many (but not all) states, a pistol may be transported legally in a motor vehicle if the pistol is unloaded, cased, and locked in the trunk. As an additional precaution, it may be advisable to disassemble the pistol and separate it from any ammunition. Many states require a permit to transport a pistol within the state, and some jurisdictions within a state may totally prohibit any transportation or possession of a pistol.

INTERSTATE TRANSPORTATION

Notwithstanding any state or local laws, a person may transport a pistol interstate provided that the person is traveling *from* any place where he or she may lawfully possess and transport the pistol *to* any other place where he or she may lawfully possess and transport the pistol. In addition, the pistol must be unloaded and locked in the trunk of the vehicle being used. If the vehicle does not have a trunk, the unloaded pistol must be in a locked container *other than the glove compartment or console.*

TRANSPORTATION ON AIRCRAFT

Federal law prohibits the carrying of any pistol, concealed or unconcealed, on or about a person's body or in carry-on luggage while aboard an aircraft. Unloaded pistols which are not accessible to a person while aboard the aircraft are usually permitted if:

1. When checking the baggage, the passenger notifies the airline that a pistol is in the baggage and that it is unloaded.
2. The baggage which contains the pistol is locked, and the passenger is the only person who has a key to it.
3. The baggage which contains the pistol will be carried in an area which is inaccessible to passengers and is not in the flight crew compartment.

It is advisable to contact the airline prior to a trip to obtain up-to-date information about these or other restrictions.

CARRYING A PISTOL ON OR ABOUT THE BODY

Carrying a pistol on or about the body, including carrying it in a readily accessible location in a vehicle, may be prohibited by state and/or local laws or may require a permit.

GENERAL PRECAUTIONS

Always use common sense and caution if planning to travel with a pistol. Remember that the person transporting a pistol is responsible for complying with all federal, state, and local laws. Ignorance of the law is not an excuse.

The Research and Information Division of the NRA's Institute for Legislative Action (ILA) has compiled free brochures on the firearm laws of the 50 states. To obtain a brochure for any state, call or write to ILA c/o The National Rifle Association of America. See the "NRA Resources" section (Appendix E) at the end of this book for the address and phone number of ILA.

Because laws pertaining to firearms change frequently, and because of the complexity and confusing nature of these laws, *it is strongly urged that a competent attorney be consulted* for complete information about such laws and their applicability to each person's situation.

The General Counsel's Office of the NRA maintains an attorney referral service for NRA members. For the name of a local attorney who has experience with firearm laws, call or write the General Counsel's Office c/o the National Rifle Association of America. See the "NRA Resources" section (Appendix E) at the end of this book for the address and phone number of the General Counsel's Office.

CHAPTER 5 REVIEW

1. Why should a pistol be cleaned?

   to be sure it will function properly & appropriately

2. When should a pistol be cleaned?

   after each firing session

3. Before starting to clean a pistol, always be absolutely certain that
   it is _*Unloaded*_ and that the action is _*Open*_ .

4. What is the most important rule that should be followed when
   storing a pistol? *No access by unauthorized people*

5. _*Ammunition*_ should NOT be present when cleaning a
   pistol.

6. To obtain complete information about firearm laws, always
   *Consult an attorney* .

NOTES

CHAPTER 6

SHOOTING FUNDAMENTALS

Now that the operation, safe handling, and care of a pistol have been explained, it is time to discuss how to shoot it. As will soon become evident, there is more to shooting than just pulling the trigger.

DETERMINING THE DOMINANT EYE

Before starting to shoot, a major question must be answered—which one of the shooter's eyes should be used for aiming?

A shooter should always aim with the dominant eye. This term is used to designate the eye which is stronger and does more work.

The dominant eye can easily be determined by performing the following exercise:

1. Extend both arms in front of the body.

2. Place the hands together, forming a small opening between them. (See Figure 24.)

3. Keep both eyes open and look through the opening at a distant object.

Figure 24

4. While continuing to look at the object, move both hands back toward the body until they touch the face.

5. The opening in the hands will now be over a single eye—the eye that is being used to see the distant object. (See Figure 25.) That's the dominant eye! This dominant eye should always be used for aiming.

Figure 25

DETERMINING THE SHOOTING HAND

A shooter must next determine which hand will be used to grip and fire a pistol. It is recommended that a shooter use the hand which is on the same side of the body as the dominant eye.

THE FUNDAMENTALS OF PISTOL SHOOTING

To shoot a pistol accurately, it is first necessary to learn and understand the six fundamentals, or basic essential components, of pistol shooting. These fundamentals are:

- Position
- Grip
- Breath Control
- Sight Alignment
- Trigger Squeeze
- Follow-through

These fundamentals must be properly performed every time a pistol is fired.

EXAMINING THE FUNDAMENTALS

Each of the above fundamentals must be examined and studied in detail:

1. Position

Proper body position is essential in order to shoot a good score. When learning any shooting position, four basic steps must be followed:

- Study the position. (Carefully review the text and examine the illustrations in this book.)
- Practice the position *without* a pistol. (Learn to put the feet, legs, body, head, and arms in the correct position without holding a pistol.)
- Practice the position *with* a pistol. (Using the correct grip described in the next section, add a pistol to the position.)
- Align the position properly with the target. (Adjust the position so that the pistol points naturally at the target.)

A variety of positions can be used when shooting a pistol. In this book, the three basic pistol positions will be studied: benchrest, two-handed standing, and one-handed standing. These positions will be described in detail in Chapter 7 and Chapter 8 of this book.

2. Grip

To achieve a proper grip:

- Keeping the gun pointed in a safe direction and the index finger off the trigger, use the non-shooting hand to place the pistol in the grip of the shooting hand. (See Figure 26.)

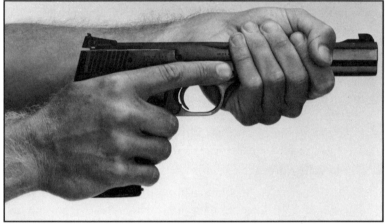

Figure 26

- Fit the "V" formed by the thumb and the index finger of the shooting hand as high as possible on the backstrap portion of the frame.

- Align the backstrap of the pistol frame with the wrist and forearm.

- Grip the pistol using the base of the thumb and the lower three fingers of the shooting hand. The pressure of the grip must be directed straight to the rear. Hold the pistol as firmly as possible, but without exerting so much pressure that the hand begins to shake.

- The index finger should *not* be placed on the trigger, but should lie along the side of the frame or on the outside of the trigger guard. Always keep the index finger off the trigger until ready to shoot.

- The thumb should lie relaxed along the side of the frame at a level above that of the index finger.
- *Uniformity* is the most important feature of a proper grip. The grip should be the same each time that the pistol is held.

Now that proper grip has been explained, this knowledge can be applied when practicing the basic pistol positions described in Chapter 7 and Chapter 8 of this book.

3. Breath Control

In order to minimize body movement, the breath must be held while firing. Before each shot, take a breath, let out enough air to be comfortable, and hold the remaining breath while firing the shot. Because firing will usually occur within a few seconds, there should be no difficulty from lack of oxygen. However, if the breath is held too long, muscle tremors may start. If tremors begin to occur, take the index finger off the trigger while keeping the muzzle pointed in a safe direction, put the gun down, relax briefly, take a few breaths, and then begin the firing cycle again.

4. Sight Alignment

Sight alignment is the relationship of the front and rear sights. The eye must be lined up with the front and rear sights and the sights positioned so that their alignment is correct.

Proper alignment of the two sights means that the top of the front sight is even with the top of the rear sight; the front sight must also be centered in the notch of the rear sight so that there is an equal amount of space on each side of the front sight. (See Figure 27.)

Figure 27

Proper sight alignment is the key to accurate shooting. Any misalignment of the front sight with the rear sight introduces an angular error that is multiplied with distance.

To fire an accurate shot, it is essential to concentrate on the *front sight*. The eye is capable of focusing clearly on only one object at a time. It cannot keep the rear sight, the front sight, and the target in focus at the same time. When the eye is focused properly, the front sight should appear sharp and clear, the rear sight should appear a little less sharp, and the target should look blurred.

A correct *sight picture* is obtained by achieving the proper sight alignment and then putting the aligned sights into their proper relationship with the target. (See Fig. 28.)

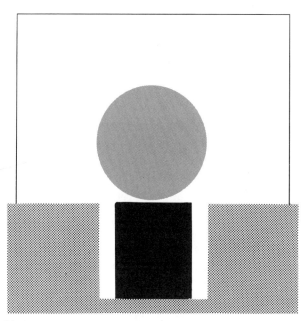

Figure 28

Don't expect to be able to hold a perfect sight picture. No pistol shooter, no matter how expert, can hold a pistol in firing position without some motion. This motion is called *arc of movement*. The very best that any shooter can do is to keep the arc of movement at a minimum—it cannot be eliminated.

Shot locations on a bullseye target are described by picturing the target as if clock numerals were surrounding it. (See Figure 29.)

The shot group shown is at 2 o'clock in the 8 ring.

Figure 29

A new shooter should hold the aligned sights at a 6 o'clock relationship to the target. (The front sight can be clearly seen against the white of the target when using a 6 o'clock hold.) Some experienced shooters prefer to use a center hold (placing the aligned sights in the center of the bullseye), but it is usually better for new shooters to use the 6 o'clock hold.

Although many good shooters aim with one eye closed, other shooters find it possible to aim the pistol with both eyes open. The dominant eye will still control aiming even though both eyes are open. This latter technique is desirable because more total light is available to the eyes and depth perception is better. It also eliminates any contortion of the face around the aiming eye.

Sometimes new shooters will have trouble closing one eye, and yet cannot sight properly with both eyes open. Temporary use of an eye patch usually solves this problem.

The front and rear sights described above are commonly referred to as *metallic sights*. The sights on some pistols are not adjustable and are known as *fixed sights*. *Target sights* can be adjusted both vertically and horizontally. Vertical adjustments will produce a change in *elevation* and move the bullet's point of impact higher or lower on the target. Horizontal adjustments, also known as *windage* adjustments, will result in a change in the bullet's impact to the left or right on the target.

The standard rule for metallic sight adjustment is: "Move the rear sight in the *same* direction that the hits on the target should move."

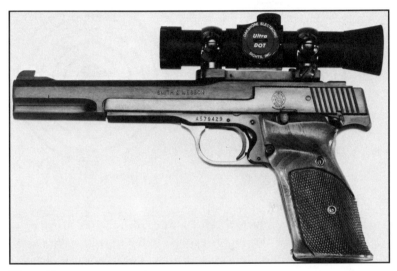

Figure 30

Two other kinds of sights can be used on a pistol: *optical sights* and *electronic sights*. An *optical sight* is a small scope (telescopic sight) mounted on a pistol. Optical sights are available with and without magnification, and use a reticle (such as crosshairs or a post) inside the scope for aiming purposes. *Electronic sights* (see Figure 30) externally resemble a scope, but use a battery-illuminated dot for aiming purposes. Both of these aiming devices eliminate the need to align a rear sight with a front sight. The reticle or the aiming dot is visually placed on the target at the desired point of bullet impact. Many shooters using these sights find it easier to aim directly at the center of the bullseye than to use a six o'clock hold. Optical and electronic sights are usually marked with windage and elevation adjustments.

A series of shots that appear together on a target is known as a *group*. Do not adjust the sights until the shots consistently form a group on the target. (See Figure 31.)

Don't worry initially about the location of the group on the target. Once the shots form a group, the location of the group on the target can be changed by adjusting the sights. (See Figure 32.)

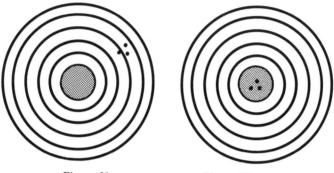

Figure 31   *Figure 32*

5. Trigger Squeeze

The term "trigger squeeze" is used in this section to explain the manner in which pressure is applied to the trigger. A variety of terms have evolved over the years to describe this process. Some of the other terms commonly used are: trigger pull, trigger control, trigger press, and trigger movement. While all of these terms are correct, the term "trigger squeeze" has been selected for use in this section because it accurately describes the smooth application of pressure required.

When ready to begin squeezing the trigger, the index finger should be located on the trigger so that the trigger is about halfway between the tip of the finger and the first joint.

The trigger must be squeezed straight to the rear in a smooth, continuous manner without disturbing the sight alignment. Once trigger squeeze has begun, it should be applied smoothly and continuously—don't speed up or slow down the pressure or apply it in a start-and-stop manner. Use the same type of pressure that would be used to squeeze a drop of liquid from a medicine dropper—a gradual, steady application of pressure until the drop finally falls. Just as it would be impossible to predict the instant that the drop of liquid would fall, it should be impossible to predict the precise instant that the gun will fire. Each shot should come as a surprise.

Trigger squeeze and sight alignment must be done simultaneously while maintaining a minimum arc of movement.

6. Follow-through

Follow-through means continuing to apply all of the shooting fundamentals throughout the delivery of the shot. In most sports, a physical action must always be completed with proper follow-through. After a golfer hits a ball, the golfer's arms should continue in the same arc as when the club first met the ball. The same principle applies to a shooter's actions. In shooting, follow-through consists of *continuing to do everything that was being done at the time the shot was fired.* The idea of follow-through is to prevent any unnecessary movement before the bullet leaves the barrel.

If the front sight is being concentrated upon when the pistol is fired, it should be possible to *call* the location of the shot on the target without actually seeing the point of impact. For example, if it is known that the front sight was improperly aligned so that it was too high above the rear sight when the shot was fired, it can be predicted that the shot hit high on the target. If the front sight was incorrectly aligned so that it was too far to the left in the notch of the rear sight, it can be predicted that the shot hit to the left on the target. Learning to call the location of the shots will help to identify shooting errors and allow appropriate corrective actions to be taken. (See Appendix D at the end of this book for a discussion of common shooting errors.)

CONCLUSION

The two most important fundamentals in pistol shooting are *sight alignment* and *trigger squeeze.* The other four fundamentals all combine to assist in achieving proper sight alignment and trigger squeeze. Remember, *all* of the fundamentals must be properly performed every time in order to shoot a pistol accurately.

65

CHAPTER 6 REVIEW

1. How can the dominant eye be determined? Explain the process.

2. The six fundamentals of pistol shooting are:

- _____Position_____
- _____Grip_____
- _____Breathing_____
- _____Sight alignment_____
- _____trigger squeeze_____
- _____follow thru_____

3. _Uniformity_____ is the most important feature of a proper grip.

4. Of the six fundamentals of pistol shooting, the two most important fundamentals are _Sight alignment_ and _trigger Squeeze_

5. If _Muscle tremors_____ begin to develop when aiming, it is best to stop, put down the pistol, relax, and take a few deep breaths.

6. Why is follow-through necessary?

N O T E S

CHAPTER 7

THE FIRST SHOOTING POSITION— BENCHREST

Now that the fundamentals of pistol shooting have been explained, it is time to take the pistol to the range and shoot it.

PISTOL CHOICES

A good gun for learning the fundamentals of pistol shooting is a .22 caliber target pistol. The fundamentals are the same regardless of caliber, and the .22 caliber target pistol offers many advantages. It makes less noise than pistols of larger caliber and it has a relatively light recoil. Ammunition is less expensive than center-fire ammunition and can be purchased in any gun store. And finally, the .22 caliber target pistol is extremely accurate.

Either a revolver or semi-automatic may be used during basic marksmanship training. However, if a revolver is chosen, it should be fired single-action whenever possible. By shooting in single-action mode, less pressure will be needed to pull the trigger, and it will be easier to concentrate on sight alignment and trigger squeeze.

TARGETS

Paper targets are recommended because the impact point of each shot can easily be seen. The blank back side of an NRA 50-foot bullseye target is a good target to use initially. The absence of a black bullseye circle will allow and enhance proper concentration on the front sight. Place the target at a distance of about 10 to 15 feet with the blank side of the target visible. Aim at the center portion of the paper, and concentrate on sight alignment and trigger squeeze.

LEARNING A SHOOTING POSITION

As discussed in Chapter 6 of this book, four basic steps should be followed when learning any shooting position:

Step 1: Study the position.

Step 2: Practice the position *without* a pistol.

Step 3: Practice the position *with* a pistol.

Step 4: Align the position properly with the target.

THE BENCHREST POSITION

The fundamentals that have been explained in this book can best be applied by using the *benchrest position* as the introduction to pistol shooting. This position permits the use of a sandbag or other object to support the hands and the pistol at the proper height, and allows the shooter to concentrate upon proper sight alignment and trigger squeeze.

The guidelines listed below for gripping and operating a pistol are for a right-handed person; left-handed persons should make appropriate adjustments to these guidelines.

GRIP AND BODY POSITION

1. Sit behind a bench or table and face the target.

2. Keeping the gun pointed in a safe direction and the index finger off the trigger, use the left hand to place the pistol in the right hand. Take a proper grip on the pistol with the right hand as explained previously on page 59 under *Grip*.

3. After correctly gripping the pistol in the right hand, place the heel of the left hand against the heel of the right hand. (See Figure 33.)

4. Rest the left thumb on top of the right thumb, and wrap the fingers of the left hand firmly around the fingers of the right hand. (See Figure 34.) CAUTION: To avoid injury when using a semi-automatic, be careful not to place the left thumb in the path that will be taken by the recoiling slide when a shot is fired.

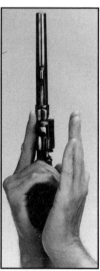

Figure 34

Figure 33

70

5. Fully extend both arms in front of the body with the hands resting on the sandbags. (See Figure 35.)

6. Position the pistol sights so that the gun naturally points at the target.

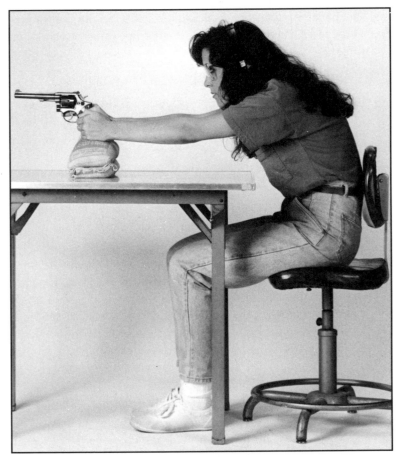

Figure 35

DRY FIRING FROM THE BENCHREST POSITION

Dry firing is the shooting of an unloaded gun. It is useful in practicing marksmanship skills, and allows a new shooter to concentrate on sight alignment and trigger squeeze without being distracted by the noise or recoil caused by firing live ammunition.

Dry firing the pistol should now be practiced using the benchrest position. This practice will provide an opportunity to become familiar with properly applying all of the fundamentals that were explained in Chapter 6, especially trigger squeeze and sight alignment. Dry firing should be practiced frequently, but always be absolutely certain that the pistol is unloaded. Obey all gun safety rules whenever handling a pistol—whether dry firing or using live cartridges.

LIVE FIRE FROM THE BENCHREST POSITION

Once that dry firing has been practiced, including the proper application of the six fundamentals of pistol shooting, it is time to fire the first shot. Obey all of the safety rules, including the wearing of eye and ear protection. Sit down at the bench with the pistol and ammunition, and carry out the following exercises:

Single-Shot Exercise

This exercise will involve the *loading and firing of one shot at a time* at the center area of a blank target. A total of five shots will be fired.

If using a revolver, load only one round into the cylinder. (Remember that the cylinder will rotate when the hammer is cocked. In order to load the chamber that will be rotated into firing position when the hammer is cocked, it is necessary to know in which direction the cylinder will turn. This direction is not the same for all revolvers.) As mentioned before, use single-action mode by cocking the hammer. Don't use double-action mode for this practice.

If using a semi-automatic, load only one cartridge into the magazine. (Don't try to bypass the magazine by manually inserting a round directly into the chamber. If the cartridge is not seated properly in the chamber, it is possible for the slide to hit and ignite the primer when the slide returns to its forward position.)

Relax, don't rush, remember to keep the sights aligned, squeeze the trigger slowly to the rear, and wait for the shot to fire. (Remember that the firing of the shot should come as a surprise.)

Fire a total of five shots. When finished, remove the magazine (if any), open the cylinder or lock the slide back, make sure the pistol is unloaded, and put the pistol down. Obeying all safety rules and range commands, retrieve the target and examine it.

Five-Round Exercise

This exercise will involve the *loading of five rounds* in the pistol. All five rounds will be fired at the center area of a blank target.

After placing a blank target downrange, load a total of five rounds into the pistol.

If using a revolver which has more than five chambers, be sure to close the cylinder with an empty chamber aligned with the barrel. As in the single-shot exercise above, be sure that when the cylinder rotates, the first loaded chamber will rotate into firing position when the hammer is cocked. The remaining four loaded chambers should rotate so that they immediately follow the first loaded chamber.

Fire a total of five rounds on the target. Concentrate on sight alignment and trigger squeeze. Relax when shooting and be sure to rest in-between each shot. Don't try to fire all five shots at once.

A good shooter must be consistent. Each of the six fundamentals of pistol shooting must be correctly performed the same way and in the same length of time *each time that a shot is fired*. By using this consistent technique, good *rhythm* can be achieved. The rhythm pattern that is developed and used in slow-fire shooting will be the same pattern that will be used in rapid-fire shooting—the pace will quicken, but the pattern will remain the same.

After firing five shots, load and fire five more rounds. The exercise is completed when a total of 10 shots have been fired. Remove the magazine (if any), open the cylinder or lock the slide back, make sure the pistol is unloaded, and put the pistol down. Obeying all safety rules and range commands, retrieve the target and examine it.

Sight Adjustment

After shot groups have been consistently achieved in practice sessions, it may be necessary to adjust the sights so that the groups will hit in the center of the target. As mentioned before, always move the rear sight in the *same* direction that the hits on the target should move. For example, if the shots are hitting high and to the right, move the rear sight down and to the left. (See Figure 36.)

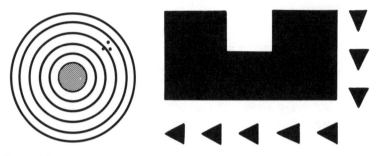

Figure 36

Some rear sights can be adjusted by using a screwdriver to turn the adjustment screws. Fixed sights should be adjusted by a competent gunsmith.

After making a sight adjustment, fire five shots to see where the bullets are impacting. If they are not hitting at the center of the target, make another sight adjustment.

PRACTICE AND SCORING THE TARGET

The above exercises will provide a basic initiation to pistol shooting. However, to improve or maintain shooting skills, it is necessary to *practice on a regular basis.*

Shooting at a bullseye target is a good way to practice marksmanship skills. The scores that are shot can be recorded and improvement can be tracked.

When scoring a bullseye target, take the value of the scoring ring area for each shot that hits within that area. If a bullet hole is touching the scoring ring itself, take the higher value. Bullet holes outside the scoring ring areas are scored as misses and have a value of zero.

Sometimes it is difficult to determine whether a bullet hole is actually touching a scoring ring. A *scoring gauge* (a device which has the same diameter as the bullet) can be inserted into the bullet hole to determine whether the hole is touching the scoring ring. (See Figure 37.)

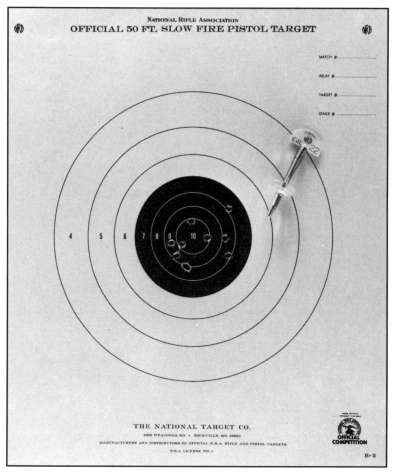

Figure 37

CHAPTER 7 REVIEW

1. What are the four basic steps for learning a shooting position?

   - *Study the position* _____ .

   - *Practice the position s a firearm* _____ .

   - *Practice w/ a firearm* _____ .

   - *Align the position w/ the target* _____ .

2. The best shooting position to use for firing the first shot is the *Bench rest* _____ position.

3. Define dry firing.
   Shooting an unloaded pistol

4. To change the impact point of a shot group on the target, the rear sight should be moved in the ___ *same* _____ direction that the hits on the target should move.

5. To improve or maintain shooting skills, it is necessary to *practice on a regular basis* _____ .

NOTES

CHAPTER 8

OTHER SHOOTING POSITIONS

Now that the fundamentals of shooting from a benchrest position have been explained, it is time to discuss two other shooting positions: the *two-handed standing position* and the *one-handed standing position*.

TWO-HANDED STANDING POSITION

Next to the benchrest position, the two-handed standing position is perhaps the easiest position for a new shooter. Both hands will be used to support the pistol when shooting, making it easy to hold the gun steady.

GRIP TECHNIQUE

1. Keeping the gun pointed in a safe direction and the index finger off the trigger, use the left hand to place the pistol in the right hand. Take a proper grip on the pistol with the right hand as explained previously on page 59 under *Grip*.

2. After correctly gripping the pistol in the right hand, there are two different methods that can be used to support the right hand:

First Method: Rest the bottom of the grip portion of the frame

Figure 38

and the heel of the right hand in the palm of the left hand. Hold the fingers of the left hand firmly up along the side of the right hand. (See Figure 38.)

Second Method: Place the heel of the left hand against the heel of the right hand. Rest the left thumb on top of the right thumb. Wrap the fingers of the left hand firmly around the fingers of the right hand. (See Figure 39. This is the same left hand support method used in the benchrest position.)

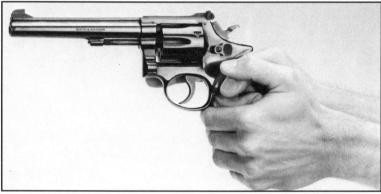

Figure 39

BODY POSITION

1. Face the target squarely with the body directly in front of the target. Position the body in the following manner:
   - Feet—shoulder width apart with body weight distributed evenly.
   - Legs—straight.
   - Back—straight.
   - Head—erect.
   - Arms—fully extended.
2. After taking the above position, use the proper two-handed grip, and bring the pistol up to eye level. The pistol should point naturally at the

Figure 40

80

center of the target. (See Figure 40.)

ONE-HANDED STANDING POSITION

The one-handed standing position is used most in competitive pistol shooting. Because only one hand is used when holding the pistol, there is not as much support as with the two-handed standing position. The one-handed position is required in many competitive events because it is more challenging than the two-handed position. However, this position can be readily mastered with practice.

GRIP TECHNIQUE

Keeping the gun pointed in a safe direction and the index finger off the trigger, use the left hand to place the pistol in the right hand. Take a proper grip on the pistol with the right hand as explained previously on page 59 under *Grip*.

BODY POSITION

1. Establish a *natural point of aim*:

   - Position the body at approximately a 45-degree angle to the target with the right side of the body closest to the target.

   - Extend the right arm toward the target.

   - Turn the head away from the target or close both eyes. Rotate the extended right arm in a small, circular pattern. Stop the motion of the arm when it feels in a comfortable, natural position.

   - Look at the target. If the hand is pointing at the center of the target, a natural point of aim has been established. (If the hand is not pointing at the center of the target, move the left foot and pivot the right foot until the hand is pointing correctly. Turn the head away from the target, and perform the arm rotation and pointing steps again. Keep repeating these steps until a natural point of aim has been established.)

2. Position the body in the following manner:

   - Feet—shoulder width apart with body weight distributed evenly.

   - Legs—straight, but not tense.

   - Body and head—comfortably erect.

- Right arm—fully extended with wrist and elbow locked in place.

- Left hand—relaxed in a pocket or comfortably hooked in a belt or waistband. (If the left hand is left dangling, it can become a distraction.)

3. After taking the above position, use the proper grip and bring the pistol up to eye level. (See Figure 41.)

Figure 41

OTHER POSITIONS

Other shooting positions can be used successfully in addition to those mentioned in this section. However, the two-handed and one-handed standing positions are more commonly used and are the easiest to learn.

C H A P T E R   8   R E V I E W

1. Briefly describe the two-handed standing shooting position.

2. Briefly describe the one-handed standing shooting position.

3. Explain how to find a natural point of aim.

CHAPTER 9

IMPROVING AND MAINTAINING SHOOTING SKILLS

Shooting is just like any other physical or mental skill—it is necessary to *practice* in order to become proficient. And, as in any sport, practice must occur on a regular basis. Don't expect to become an expert shooter overnight—but by staying with it and faithfully following the fundamentals explained in this book, progress can be quickly achieved.

The strong foundation of knowledge and skill acquired by study and practice can be built upon by becoming involved in organized shooting activities. Examples of some of these activities are described below.

QUALIFICATION SHOOTING

An exciting way to improve shooting skills is through participation in NRA qualification programs. These programs allow a shooter to demonstrate the ability to achieve certain minimum scores on NRA-designated courses of fire.

Shooters can advance at their own pace while being rewarded with certificates and brassards at each step of the program. After successfully meeting the criteria for an award level, shooters advance to the next level.

Awards are presented for achievement at the Pro-Marksman, Marksman, Marksman 1ST Class, Sharpshooter, Expert, and Distinguished Expert skill levels.

See Appendix C of this book for additional information on the NRA Marksmanship Qualification Program for pistol shooters.

COMPETITIVE SHOOTING

Many people discover that their marksmanship skills improve rapidly when shooting in competition. The NRA Competitive Shooting Division sponsors competitive shooting tournaments and leagues that are held throughout the country. The NRA establishes rules for shooting competitions and sanctioned tournaments, and maintains a computerized record system for competitors who have received an NRA classification. The NRA also publishes *Shooting Sports USA* which is devoted to the competitive shooter and contains lists of NRA-sponsored tournaments. For information on competitive shooting, contact the NRA Competitive Shooting Division.

INSTRUCTION

The National Rifle Association has more than 42,000 certified instructors located throughout America teaching basic marksmanship and firearms courses. The types of courses offered by NRA Certified Instructors are:

- Basic Pistol Shooting
- Basic Rifle Shooting

- Basic Shotgun Shooting
- Basic Muzzleloading Pistol
- Basic Muzzleloading Rifle
- Basic Muzzleloading Shotgun
- Home Firearm Safety
- Personal Protection
- Reloading

The NRA's Training Department can provide lists of local NRA Certified Instructors.

In addition, the NRA offers a series of inexpensive books, films, and tapes that describe and illustrate the fundamentals of shooting.

SHOOTING WITH FRIENDS

Many shooters pursue their interests through organized shooting clubs. More than 13,000 local clubs are enrolled or affiliated with the NRA and offer a wide range of recreational and competitive pistol shooting activities—many geared for the beginning shooter. These clubs can also be a source of new social opportunities, and provide opportunities to meet others who share an interest in safety and marksmanship skills. For information on local shooting clubs, contact the NRA Clubs and Associations Department.

CHAPTER 9 REVIEW

1. Describe some ways to improve and maintain shooting skills.

2. What is the difference between qualification shooting and competitive shooting?

3. How can a local NRA Certified Instructor be found?

N O T E S

APPENDIX A

BUYING A PISTOL

Before buying a pistol, it is essential to first understand the various laws concerning the purchase, ownership, possession, use, carrying, and transportation of pistols. These laws vary widely from community to community and state to state. Each gun owner has both a personal responsibility and a legal obligation to know and obey these laws. Penalties for gun violations can be severe.

WHAT TYPE OF PISTOL?

The type of pistol to be selected should be based upon a number of factors, including the intended use for the pistol (target shooting, hunting, personal protection, etc.), the cost of the pistol and its ammunition, the amount of recoil, and the ease of handling.

A good handgun for learning the fundamentals of pistol shooting is a .22 caliber target pistol. These pistols, available in revolver or semi-automatic models, are accurate, have light recoil, and use inexpensive ammunition. For other types of shooting, a different caliber pistol may be more appropriate.

In general, revolvers are well-suited for hunting, but can also be used for personal protection. Semi-automatics are a good choice for shooting in competitions that include timed fire and rapid fire stages.

Be sure to thoroughly investigate all of the possible choices before reaching a final decision. Ask the advice of a knowledgeable person. Talk to a reputable gun dealer. Obtain gun catalogs to review by writing or calling gun manufacturers.

FINAL CHECKLIST

- Determine the intended use for the pistol. Will it have a single or multi-purpose use? Will it be used for competitive shooting, hunting, and/or personal protection? Should it have fixed or adjustable sights? What will be the best caliber and barrel length for the intended use?

- Decide how much money to spend. While it may be necessary to stay within a budget, don't economize on quality.

- Is the ammunition for the pistol easily available? How much shooting will be done? How much does the ammunition cost?
- Study the various makes and models of pistols.
- Seek the advice of a knowledgeable person.
- Be sure that the pistol fits the hand properly. Be able to obtain a correct grip on the pistol and be sure that the index finger can easily reach the trigger.
- Consider the pistol's simplicity of operation and ease of cleaning.
- Obtain information about the pistol's manufacturer. Are parts and service readily available? Is it likely that parts and service will be available in the future?
- Does the pistol have a record of trouble-free dependability?
- Does the pistol have a warranty and guarantee? Review these documents carefully.
- Purchase the pistol from a reputable dealer.

APPENDIX B

AIR PISTOL TYPES AND OPERATION

An air pistol is a type of gun which forces a projectile, e.g., a BB or pellet, through its barrel by use of compressed air or carbon dioxide gas (CO_2). A powder charge is not used in this type of pistol.

Air pistols are good starter guns and also offer an opportunity to improve shooting skills through frequent practice–they can be used as an inexpensive training tool in a variety of locations. The same shooting fundamentals apply to air pistols as to other types of pistols, and because air pistols make relatively little noise and are less powerful than other pistols, a range can usually be set up in a home or back yard.

TYPES OF AIR PISTOLS

The two types of air pistols available today are the *spring-piston* pistol and the *pneumatic* pistol.

Spring-Piston Pistols

The spring-piston pistol is powered by a *compression spring* that is manually cocked. This spring is released when the trigger is squeezed, and drives a *piston* forward. The piston compresses the air in front of it, and this air forces the projectile out of the barrel. The air is not stored in the gun; air compression occurs due to the movement of the piston after the trigger is pulled.

Two popular types of spring-piston pistols are the *break-barrel* pistol and the *sidelever* pistol. In the break-barrel pistol, the compression spring is cocked by pulling the barrel straight down. In the sidelever pistol, the compression spring is cocked by pulling to the rear a lever located on the side of the pistol.

Pneumatic Pistols

The pneumatic pistol uses the principle of *stored* compressed air or gas.

Some pistols use a lever or a pivoting barrel to pump and compress air into a storage reservoir or chamber. In other pistols, a small disposable metal cylinder containing compressed *carbon dioxide gas (CO$_2$)* is inserted into the gun. (Models that use refillable gas cylinders are also available.) In some pistols, compressed air from an external source (such as a large scuba-type tank or an air pump) is used to fill an internal reservoir in the gun.

PROJECTILES FOR AIR PISTOLS

The two basic types of air pistol projectiles are *BBs* and *pellets*.

BBs are round projectiles made from either steel or lead. BBs can be used for target shooting or for plinking (informal shooting at a variety of targets).

Pellets are projectiles pressed from lead and are usually .177 or .22 caliber. Pellets are available in two basic body styles: the *hourglass* (or *diabolo*) style and the *cylindrical* style. The shape of the pellet head will vary according to the purpose for which it will be used. For example, a wadcutter pellet is designed for paper target competition. It has a flat head which will cut a sharp-edged, full diameter hole in a paper target.

SAFETY

Although air pistols are not firearms and do not utilize a cartridge, they are nevertheless guns and should always be treated as such. Injury and damage can occur from using air pistols improperly. Always be sure to observe all of the gun safety rules, including the use of eye protection.

APPENDIX C

NRA PISTOL MARKSMANSHIP QUALIFICATION PROGRAM

The NRA Marksmanship Qualification Programs provide an opportunity to shoot for nationally recognized NRA qualification awards. Any range may be used, including informal ranges, provided that all safety requirements are met. There are three types of pistol courses available.

Progression is self-paced, scores are challenging but attainable, and patches, medals, and certificates are available to recognize and reward each step of your skill development. Whichever course of fire you prefer, pistol qualification shooting will provide many hours of fun and enjoyment while developing pistol sport skills.

ADMINISTRATION: Acquiring qualification ratings is done on the honor system. Qualification shooting can be a self-administered activity, or it can be administered by parents, leaders, coaches, and instructors as part of a club or group program.

ELIGIBILITY: NRA Pistol Qualification courses of fire are open to everyone.

RATINGS: Novice shooters must earn ratings progressively. The required number of targets or courses do not have to be fired consecutively or in the same session.

SCORES: Scores fired to obtain one rating may not be used to earn another rating. Scores fired in practice sessions, leagues, or in competition may be applied toward qualification ratings.

SIGHTS: Metallic, telescopic, or electronic sights are permitted with the exception of any sight that projects an image onto the target.

RULES: Except where specific exceptions are made, official NRA Pistol Rules apply. Obtain a copy of the rule book before firing for qualification.

GUNS: Any rimfire or centerfire semi-automatic pistol or revolver in compliance with NRA Pistol Rules may be used.

Fired targets should not be sent to the NRA. They may be kept by the shooter as souvenirs or retained by the program administrator.

NRA STAFF: NRA staff is available to help you get started and answer any questions you may have. A booklet is available which provides the scores required for all pistol, rifle, and shotgun Marksmanship Qualification Programs currently offered. Call the NRA Qualification Program Coordinator at (703) 267-1591.

APPENDIX D

Most shooters' problems result from the failure to properly apply the two most important shooting fundamentals: sight alignment and trigger squeeze. However, other factors may also cause a shooter to have problems in properly delivering a shot to the target.

Illustrated in this section are eight common errors committed by many pistol shooters. Study the bullseye target pictures and the accompanying text carefully—the solution to a troublesome shooting problem might be found here. (Be aware that explanations other than the ones suggested here may also apply to the illustrated problem.) Shooters who are having problems should seek advice from a pistol instructor or coach.

The shooting situations pictured below assume that the pistol and ammunition are functioning correctly, that the pistol sights are adjusted properly, and that the shooter is right-handed. (The shot groups for a left-handed shooter will appear on the opposite side from the shot groups illustrated.)

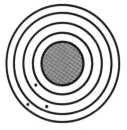

FIGURE 1:

This pattern is caused when the shooter jerks the trigger, causing the front sight to dip low and to the left before the bullet leaves the barrel. To correct this type of error, the trigger must be slowly SQUEEZED until the shot fires, being careful while squeezing not to disturb the sight alignment and sight picture.

FIGURE 2:

This target shows the effect of "riding the recoil"—the shooter anticipates the recoil and makes the pistol recoil before it really happens. This type of pattern can also be caused by improper follow-through: the shooter releases the trigger finger too soon and may flip the finger forward, causing the front sight to rise to the left. Errors of this nature will usually produce shots in the 9:30–12 o'clock zone.

FIGURE 3:

This pattern is created when the shooter does not properly place the index finger on the trigger. In such cases, the shooter has a tendency to squeeze the trigger at an angle instead of straight to the rear. This improper squeeze causes the muzzle to shift to the left, with the shots striking in the 8:30–9:30 o'clock zone.

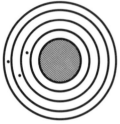

FIGURE 4:

In this example, the shooter has "heeled" the shots high on the target. This error is caused by anticipating the shot and, at the last moment before firing, giving the pistol a slight push with the heel of the hand. The front sight moves up to the right and the bullets strike the target in the 1–2:30 o'clock zone.

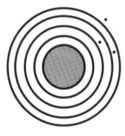

FIGURE 5:

The shots in this target are strung over to the 2:30–3 o'clock zone, and are caused when the shooter "thumbs" the pistol. Just as the shot begins, the shooter pushes the right thumb against the side of the frame, causing the aligned sights to move to the right.

FIGURE 6:

The shot string shown here in the 5–6:30 o'clock area is caused when the shooter "breaks" the wrist—another form of anticipation. The shooter expects the pistol to recoil at a known instant and tries to fight or control this anticipated recoil by cocking the wrist downward. The shooter may subconsciously believe that the recoil can be lessened by holding the wrist down. This shot group can also be caused by a shooter who relaxes too soon.

FIGURE 7:

The above target illustrates what happens when a shooter's grip tightens as the trigger is squeezed. This target area is known as the "lobster" area—just as a lobster's claw clamps together, the shooter's hand clamps or snatches at the last second. This movement causes the front sight to dip low and to the right, pushing the shots to the 3:30–5 o'clock zone.

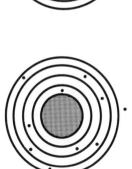

FIGURE 8:

This pattern is frequently produced by a beginning shooter. A new shooter usually does not consistently repeat one particular error, but instead commits many different errors. The result is a target with shots scattered in many places. Such a target may be caused by the shooter's inconsistency: changing the grip between shots, focusing on the target instead of the front sight on some shots, failing to align the sights properly, etc. This pattern could also be caused by a new shooter's lack of holding strength and a resultant large arc of movement. To improve pistol skills, shooters should carefully and periodically review the fundamentals of pistol shooting to determine if they are violating any basic principles.

APPENDIX E

NRA RESOURCES

THE NRA IS HERE TO HELP - WE'RE AS NEAR AS
THE TELEPHONE OR MAILBOX!

To contact the NRA for assistance or additional information, please direct
all inquiries to:

National Rifle Association of America
11250 Waples Mill Road
Fairfax, Va. 22030

Phone: (703) 267-1000
(Main Switchboard)

For questions relating to specific NRA divisions, send mail inquiries
directly to the attention of those divisions at the above address, or use the
following telephone numbers:

Community Service Programs Division

General Information. . . . . (703) 267-1560
Communications Department. . . . . (703) 267-1587
Eddie Eagle GunSafe® Program. . . . . (800) 231-0752
NRA Shooting Education Update. . . . . (703) 267-1577
Women's Programs Department. . . . . (800) 861-1166

Competitive Shooting Division

General information. . . . . (703) 267-1450
Bianchi Cup information . . . . (703) 267-1486
National Matches (Camp Perry) information . . . . (703) 267-1451
Collegiate Shooting Department . . . . (703) 267-1473
Disabled Shooting Department. . . . . (703) 267-1495
Pistol/Action Shooting Department . . . . (703) 267-1451
Rifle Department . . . . (703) 267-1456
Silhouette/Black Powder Department. . . . . (703) 267-1474
Tournament Operations Department. . . . . (703) 267-1459
Tournament Reporting Department . . . . (703) 267-1454
Volunteers Department. . . . . (703) 267-1485

Education and Training Division
General information. . . . . (703) 267-1470
Training Program information
   (automated voice mail). (703) 267-1430
Coach Programs. . . . . (703) 267-1401
Gunsmithing . . . . (703) 267-1412
Hunter Services Department . . . . (703) 267-1500
Marksmanship Qualification Program and Courses . . . (703) 267-1591
Training Department . . . . (703) 267-1431
Youth Programs Department . . . . (703) 267-1596

Field Operations Division
General information. . . . . (703) 267-1340
Clubs and Associations Department. . . . . (703) 267-1343
Friends of NRA. . . . . (703) 267-1361
Range Development. . . . . (703) 267-3808

General Counsel's Office. . . . . (703) 267-1250

Institute for Legislative Action
Research and Information . . . . (703) 267-1180

Members' Insurance
Life, Accident, & Health . . . . (800) 247-7989

Membership Division
All locations except Virginia . . . . (800) NRA-3888
In Virginia . . . . (703) 267-3888

National Firearms Museum
Gun Collecting . . . . (703) 267-1600
Museum . . . . (703) 267-1600

Other NRA resources can be contacted at the following addresses and phone numbers:

Club Liability Insurance
Lockton Risk Services
For information. . . . . (877) 487-5407

Sales Department

NRA Sales Department
P.O. Box 5000
Kearneysville, WV 25430-5000
Information and credit card charges . . . . (800) 336-7402

Technical Questions

Receiving answers to technical questions is a privilege reserved for NRA members. (A non-member may submit a question if the inquiry is accompanied by a membership application.) Each question must be in the form of a letter addressed to:

Dope Bag
NRA Publications
11250 Waples Mill Road
Fairfax, Va. 22030

Each inquiry must contain the NRA member's code line from his or her membership card or from the mailing label on the *American Rifleman* or *American Hunter* magazine. Inquiries must be limited to one specific question per letter. Questions regarding the value of any type of firearm will not be accepted. In addition, each inquiry must include a stamped, self-addressed, legal-size envelope. No technical questions will be answered by telephone or by FAX.

APPENDIX F

NRA PUBLICATIONS & VIDEOS

The items listed below are some of the various materials available from the National Rifle Association of America (NRA). To inquire about any of these items or to place an order, contact the NRA Sales Department by telephoning (800) 336-7402, Weekdays 8:30 a.m. - 11:00 p.m., Saturday & Sunday 10:00 a.m. - 6:00 p.m., Eastern time.

National Rifle Association Gun Safety Rules - An illustrated, multi-color, eight-panel brochure (which unfolds to feature a 16" x 17" gun rules safety poster on the reverse side) explaining the three fundamental rules of gun safety, plus rules for using and storing a gun. Item # 14080.

A Parent's Guide to Gun Safety - A brochure explaining parental responsibilities regarding gun safety for children, when and what to teach a child, and basic gun safety rules. Item # 12850.

Smart & Safe: Handling Your Firearm - Geared for new gun owners, this comprehensive booklet emphasizes responsibility, safe gun handling and an overview of the various types of guns and their actions. Item # 11532.

Firearm Safety and the Hunter - An illustrated, 6-panel brochure explaining safe gun handling in the field and describing field safety rules for hunters. Item # 07430.

The Basics of Rifle Shooting - An illustrated, soft-cover handbook explaining rifle parts and terms, types of ammunition, operation of various rifle actions, safety, cleaning, storage, fundamentals of rifle shooting, shooting positions, and improvement of shooting skills. Item # 13180.

NRA Junior Rifle Shooting - An illustrated, soft-cover book specifically designed for young shooters. The book not only covers such topics as gun safety, rifle parts, and shooting equipment, but also describes in detail the various rifle shooting positions. Training tips and suggestions for improving shooting skills are also discussed. Item # 09450.

The Basics of Shotgun Shooting - An illustrated, soft-cover hand book explaining shotgun parts and terms, types of ammunition, operation of various shotgun actions, safety, cleaning, storage, fundamentals of shotgun shooting, and improvement of shooting skills. Item # 13360.

The Skeeters' Guide - A companion for beginning Skeet Shooters. Jam packed with QuickTips to help new shooters learn the game, understand the jargon, and know what to do on all eight shooting stations. 39 pages, Soft-cover. Item # 09180.

Fundamentals of Gun Safety (VHS Format Videotape) - A 10-minute videotape, narrated by Steve Kanaly and Susan Howard of the TV series *Dallas,* explaining the basics of firearm safety with special emphasis on NRA's three fundamental gun safety rules. Suitable for both teenagers and adults. Item # 11560.

The Eddie Eagle GunSafe® Program - The Eddie Eagle GunSafe® Program was developed to teach children what to do if they find a gun in an unsupervised situation: "STOP! Don't Touch. Leave the Area. Tell an Adult." **The Eddie Eagle GunSafe® Program Brochure** provides an overview of the program and explains program materials. Item # EE 12350.

Limited quantities of program materials are provided free to schools and law enforcement agencies on first time orders. Youth groups and civic organizations may order the materials for a nominal charge.

For more information on this program, call The Eddie Eagle GunSafe® Program toll-free number at 1-800-231-0752, or visit their Web site at: www.nrahq.org/safety/eddie.

APPENDIX G

FACTS ABOUT THE NRA

Established in 1871, the National Rifle Association of America (NRA) is a non-profit organization supported entirely by membership fees and by donations from public-spirited citizens.

The membership roster of the NRA has included seven Presidents of the United States, two Chief Justices of the U.S. Supreme Court, and many of America's outstanding diplomats, military leaders, members of Congress, and other public officials.

Originally formed to promote marksmanship training, the NRA has since reached out to establish a wide variety of activities, ranging from gun safety programs for children and adults to gun collecting and gunsmithing. Hundreds of thousands of law enforcement personnel have received training from NRA Certified Instructors in the firearms skills needed to protect themselves and the public. In addition, clubs enrolled or affiliated with the NRA exist in communities across the nation, teaching youths and adults gun safety, marksmanship, and responsibility while also providing recreational activities.

The NRA cooperates with federal agencies, all branches of the U.S. Armed Forces, and state and local governments that are interested in training and safety programs.

The basic goals of the NRA are to:

- Protect and defend the Constitution of the United States, especially in regard to the Second Amendment right of the individual citizen to keep and bear arms.
- Promote public safety, law and order, and the national defense.
- Train citizens and members of law enforcement agencies and the armed forces in the safe handling and efficient use of firearms.
- Foster and promote the shooting sports at local, state, regional, national, and international levels.
- Promote hunter safety and proper wildlife management.

The NRA does not receive any appropriations from Congress, nor is it a trade organization. It is not affiliated with any gun or ammunition manufacturers or with any businesses which deal in guns or ammunition.

For additional information about the NRA, including programs, publications, and membership, contact:

National Rifle Association of America
11250 Waples Mill Road
Fairfax, Va. 22030

Phone: (703) 267-1000
(Main Switchboard)

TO JOIN NRA TODAY, OR FOR ADDITIONAL INFORMATION REGARDING MEMBERSHIP, PLEASE CALL 1-800-NRA-3888. YOUR MEMBERSHIP DUES CAN BE CHARGED TO VISA, MASTERCARD, AMERICAN EXPRESS, OR DISCOVER.

APPENDIX H

NRA SHORT-TERM GUNSMITHING SCHOOLS

NRA-affiliated gunsmithing schools offer short-term summer courses (most are approximately five days in length) on many interesting subjects to include: accurizing Model 1911 pistols, design and repair of double-action semi-automatic pistols and revolvers, pistolsmithing single-action revolvers, bluing, parkerizing, etc.

There are currently five NRA-affiliated gunsmithing schools. For information, contact the schools listed below or call NRA Headquarters at (703) 267-1412.

Lassen Community College
Highway 139
P.O. Box 3000
Susanville, CA 96130
(530) 251-8800

Montgomery Community College
P.O. Box 787
Troy, NC 27371
(910) 576-6222

Murray State College
1100 South Murray
Tishomingo, OK 73460
(580)-371-2371

Trinidad State Junior College
600 Prospect
Box 407
Trinidad, CO 81082
(719) 846-5616

Yavapai College
1100 E. Sheldon St.
Prescott, AZ 86301
(928) 776-2348

GLOSSARY

ACP: An abbreviation for Automatic Colt Pistol. Used in conjunction with caliber designations. Example: a .45 ACP cartridge.

Action: A series of moving parts that allow a firearm to be loaded, fired, and unloaded.

Backstrap: The rear, vertical portion of the pistol frame that lies between the grip panels.

Bore: The inside of the barrel of a firearm.

Caliber: The diameter of a projectile or the distance between the lands in the bore of a firearm.

Cartridge: A complete single unit of ammunition including the projectile, case, primer, and powder charge.

Center-fire: A type of cartridge which has the primer centrally located in the base of the case.

Chamber: The part of a firearm in which a cartridge is contained at the instant of firing.

Cylinder: The part of a revolver that holds ammunition in individual chambers that are rotated into firing position by the action of the trigger or hammer.

Double-action: A type of pistol action in which squeezing the trigger will both cock and release the hammer or internal firing mechanism.

Dry firing: The shooting of an unloaded gun.

Ejector: The part of a pistol which ejects an empty cartridge case or a cartridge from the gun.

Grooves: The shallow, spiral cuts in a bore that together with the lands make up the rifling in the bore of a barrel.

Hammer: The part of a pistol that pivots on an axis at the rear of the frame, and, when activated by the trigger, causes the firing pin to strike a cartridge.

Hangfire: A perceptible delay in the ignition of a cartridge after the primer has been struck by the firing pin.

Misfire: A failure of a cartridge to fire after the primer has been struck by the firing pin.

Muzzle: The front end of the barrel from which a projectile exits.

Parabellum: Taken from Latin, this term translates as "prepare for war." During World War I, the Deutsche Waffen und Munitionsfabrik (DWM) used this term for its Luger pistol and a machine gun. Parabellum is used today as a synonym for Luger to identify 7.65mm and 9mm Luger ammunition.

Patridge sight: A type of sight designed by E.E. Patridge in the late 1800s, generally used on handguns. It has a rear sight with a square notch, and a front sight consisting of a thick blade that is flat on top.

Pistol: A gun that has a short barrel and can be held, aimed, and fired with one hand.

+P (Plus P): Cartridges which are loaded to higher pressures than standard ammunition.

+P+ (Plus P Plus): Cartridges which are loaded to higher pressures than +P ammunition.

Plinking: Informal shooting at a variety of targets.

Revolver: A pistol that has a rotating cylinder containing a number of firing chambers. The action of the trigger or hammer will line up a chamber with the barrel and firing pin.

Rifling: Spiral lands and grooves in the barrel bore that provide a stabilizing spin to a bullet so that it will be more accurate in flight.

Rimfire: A cartridge which has the chemical compound of the primer located inside the rim of the case.

Round: Another term for a cartridge.

Semi-automatic: A pistol that fires a single cartridge each time the trigger is pulled, and which automatically extracts and ejects the empty case and inserts a new cartridge into the chamber.

Single-action: A type of pistol action in which pulling the trigger will release the hammer.

Sights: Mechanical, optical, or electronic devices used to aim a pistol.

Squib load: A cartridge which develops less than normal pressure or velocity after ignition of the cartridge.

INDEX

115